# WATERGATE, POLITICS, AND THE LEGAL PROCESS

∽

Alexander M. Bickel, *Chairman*

∽

Charles S. Hyneman
Richard M. Scammon
Harry H. Wellington
Aaron Wildavsky
James Q. Wilson
Ralph K. Winter, Jr.

An AEI Round Table held on 13 and 14 March 1974
at the
American Enterprise Institute for Public Policy Research
Washington, D.C.

ISBN 0-8447-2046-1
LIBRARY OF CONGRESS CATALOG CARD NO. L.C. 74-77431

*PRINTED IN UNITED STATES OF AMERICA*

# CONTENTS

## PART I

## PART II

# PART I

Alexander M. Bickel, *Chairman*

Charles S. Hyneman
Richard M. Scammon
Aaron Wildavsky
James Q. Wilson
Ralph K. Winter, Jr.

ALEXANDER M. BICKEL, Chancellor Kent professor of law, Yale Law School: All along the spectrum of opinion and emotion about Watergate, over the entire distance from embattled defensiveness to unqualified moral outrage, from the President himself to pickets calling for his resignation or impeachment or preferably both—from one end of this spectrum of opinion and emotion to the other, and at most points in between, there seems to be fairly general agreement on one proposition. That is, that Watergate has demonstrated the need for institutional and procedural reform in the structure of American politics and government.

Now, there isn't universal agreement, of course, on the nature of the reforms that are needed. Proposals are many and varied. But there is a remarkable consensus that reforms are needed and that Watergate has shown what the defects in our system are.

We are here to discuss what may usefully be done, what reforms seem wise and appropriate—not only because Watergate has demonstrated a need for them, but also because Watergate has created a climate of opinion that is hospitable to change and it would be foolish to disregard that fact. And we're also here to ask, we hope with some detachment, the question that so often gets lost in the excitement: namely, whether deep-cutting reforms are really needed, whether we should rush into fundamental alterations in the structure and procedures of American politics and government, or whether we may not be engulfed by or in danger of being engulfed by an overreaction to

Watergate. The cry is: "Don't just sit there, do something." Perhaps on some matters the better advice, as someone once said to the late agitated actress, Zazu Pitts, may be: "Don't just do something, sit there."

We've divided our topic into five subtopics or subjects and we'll discuss them at two Round Tables of which this is the first.

Tonight we're going to begin with the problem of campaign financing and spending, discussing chiefly the questions: should expenditures by candidates be limited, and should there be public financing of campaigns? Then, since reform of campaign financing and spending would, of course, radically alter presidential politics, we thought it logical to go from that to a second topic, namely: should there be changes in the structure and function of the presidency?

Tomorrow night we will deal with three subjects: first, the President's powers and functions in the area of domestic and national security, issues such as wiretapping and other emergency powers; second, the problem of politics infringing on the Department of Justice, on the administration of justice, and the possible need for special prosecutors; and, finally, some matters of immediate interest, such as the reach of the impeachment power, its relationship to claims of executive privilege, and the accommodations that may be necessary between the impeachment power and the rights of defendants in criminal trials.

NOW, THE CENTERPIECE of our discussion— really the excuse for our being here—is the study by Mr. Ralph Winter entitled *Watergate and the Law.** So, on our first issue of campaign spending, as on the other questions that we will discuss, I will turn first to Mr. Winter to lead us off.

* Ralph K. Winter, Jr., *Watergate and the Law: Political Campaigns and Presidential Power* (Washington, D.C.: American Enterprise Institute, 1974).

RALPH K. WINTER, JR., professor of law, Yale Law School: Thanks, Alex. I think the questions of limitations on candidate expenditures and limitations on individual contributions ought to be taken up separately, because they raise very different problems. Virtually every bill now before the Congress, and in the judgment of a lot of people every bill that is likely to pass, contains limitations on candidate expenditures. We ought to take that first, therefore, since it seems to be a linchpin of all possible legislation.

The rationale for limiting candidate expenditures is not entirely clear. While there is a great deal of rhetoric about the cost of campaigns, it's not clear how one judges that campaigns cost too much. Most of the evidence seems to indicate that campaign budgets are not particularly excessive when compared with commercial advertising budgets.

The principal justification, I think, for limits on candidate expenditures goes to the incentive question— to the idea that if you limit how much a candidate will spend, you will also limit the incumbent officeholder's power or incentive to go to people and ask them for contributions with the idea that some benefits or detriment might or might not be given in the future. That is to say, you decrease his incentive to go out and raise money in illegal or unethical ways.

Now, there are a number of objections, very cogent objections, to limitations on candidate expenditures. The first concerns the problem of incumbency. The fact is that, in any campaign, money is much more useful to the candidate who is less known, whose ideas have been circulated less widely, than to the candidate who is well known and who represents the prevailing viewpoint. Generally that means that money is far more useful to challengers than to incumbents, so that there is the danger that if we limit total expenditures by candidates, the limits will be set so low that incumbents will be given an advantage over challengers, an extra advantage indeed. At the moment, incumbents have an enormous advantage anyway

5

because of subsidies from the government—office staffs and the like—and because they have access to the media.

Let me give you an example of this. The bill reported out by the Senate Rules Committee and sponsored by most of the groups which now clamor for a campaign reform—it's sometimes called the Kennedy-Scott bill—provides for public financing up to a maximum of $21 million per presidential candidate. That $21 million is all that a candidate would be able to spend. Now, imagine a campaign in which an incumbent President eligible for reelection is faced by a challenger who has only $21 million to spend. McGovern, after all, raised $38 million. The incumbent President has access to Air Force I, can hold news conferences, can do all kinds of things to run a so-called nonpolitical campaign. If this bill is passed, he would just devastate the challenger, who would have totally inadequate funds.

It seems to me that this kind of a proposal, which we hear is a reform emanating from Watergate, would be a very cruel irony, because the effect of the proposal would be to increase the power of incumbent Presidents enormously—exactly the wrong lesson, one would think, to be learned from Watergate.

The incumbency problem must be emphasized, because the only people who can vote limits on candidate expenditures are incumbent politicians. It is really too much to expect, therefore, that Congress will enact limitations which will not seriously deprive challengers of the opportunity to wage a fair campaign. For instance, it is being said that it takes $100,000 to unseat an incumbent member of the House of Representatives.

MR. BICKEL: Can you be sure?

MR. WINTER: Well, one reason you might be sure is that if you look at all of the proposals coming from the House, $90,000 is the highest limit—

MR. BICKEL: I meant, is it guaranteed?

MR. WINTER: No, it's not guaranteed, so you can keep your fortune intact, Alex.

The second issue about limits on candidate expenditures is that, to be effective, they must limit everyone's ability to spend money on a political campaign. That is to say, if you want to limit candidate Scammon's expenditures, you would have to make sure that his wealthy supporter, Mr. Bickel, will not go out and independently wage a campaign for him. You would also have to have some kind of prohibition so that so-called independent committees won't be set up to run campaigns.

This means that every law putting a limit on candidate expenditures also would have to have some kind of device which effectively prevented other expenditures or advertising expenditures by people not working on the candidate's behalf. I'll give you an example: if the American Civil Liberties Union, for instance, wanted to run an add in the *New York Times* listing congressmen who were pro-busing, under the Kennedy-Scott bill and under present law, it would be effectively restrained from doing so.

Now, it seems to me that raises a very, very serious constitutional problem under the First Amendment, because it is a flat prohibition on peaceful political speech. It would be rather unprecedented in our history, I think, and is probably unconstitutional.

I would like also to add that I don't regard this as a legal technicality. It seems to me that the independent, private advertising in a campaign may, in fact, bring issues out more clearly than would be done if everything were left to advertising firms working for the candidates. Indeed, it may provide some flavor to the campaign and information that we would not otherwise get. So it does seem to me that limitations on candidate expenditures raise very, very serious problems, problems that, as of this day, are so serious that we ought not enact the limitations.

MR. BICKEL: Just to throw in one point, I'm very much of your view on the constitutional issue and I think it is just an inevitable one: without limiting other peoples' expenditures, you don't have a real limit; if you do limit them, it's a very serious constitutional issue.

But on the incumbency problem, I just wonder if that's not a little overemphasized. First of all, to make a very simplistic point—not necessarily naive, but simple —if it's a real problem, why can't I set a different limit, a lower limit, on expenditures by an incumbent than on expenditures by a challenger?

MR. WINTER: Well, I think that's a good question.

MR. BICKEL: You say Congress won't do it.

MR. WINTER: Well, I think that's a good question because it does point up the problem. If we're really interested in fairness—if all of the cries for reform and all of the rhetoric about cleansing the political process are true— why has not one single proposal seriously suggested that challengers be given more to spend and have higher spending limits than incumbents?

MR. BICKEL: Because you and I are the only high-minded people in the room.

CHARLES S. HYNEMAN, fellow, Woodrow Wilson International Center for Scholars: Well, if one pushed that kind of a proposition, might he not then, with equally good reason, say that the man who is very attractive on TV ought to be helped less by monetary funds than the person who doesn't go over very well on TV? So that if a Charles Lindbergh were to run for President, he ought not to be allowed to spend a cent because no other candidate could collect the amount of money necessary to catch up with him.

MR. BICKEL: But incumbency is not an innate quality. It is a little different.

MR. WINTER: It's not only not an innate quality. What we're raising is the question of self-interest—that these so-called reforms surrounded with a rhetoric of high-mindedness are being enacted by people who have an enor-

8

mous self-interest in the regulations that they contain. And there isn't anything that is happening to control that self-interest. Asking the Congress to regulate this process creates a conflict of interest problem, really, and has nothing to do with Charles Lindbergh.

MR. HYNEMAN: Well, I think one could well make the point that an elective body ought not to have any authority to control the elective process whatever. But we've not arranged in this constitutional system for any other authority to do that.

MR. BICKEL: Oh yes we have—on apportionment, where we have given it to the courts. We've done exactly that on the ground that presumably there is too much self-interest there.

But, again, the self-interest problem is soluble. If that's the heart of the problem, then we ought to try and arrange some kind of a commission—as we have with congressmen's salaries—some kind of a commission to make a proposal and Congress would have sixty days to vote it down or whatever. I mean, we should take the matter effectively out of the real political process in Congress.

I think the incumbency problem and the problem of expecting action from self-interested people are soluble problems. They are there, but they don't seem to me decisive against the proposal.

JAMES Q. WILSON, professor of government, Harvard University: I'm not sure the problem is as easily disposed of as that. If you look at the history of Congress, you will notice a striking reduction in the proportion of freshmen —newly elected congressmen—who are returned in each session. Some years it goes up; some years it goes down. But the turnover of congressmen is much less today than it was 20 or 50 or certainly 100 years ago.

There are many reasons for this, but one of the reasons is the substantial enlargement of the institutionalized congressional office—local staffs in the home district, staffs in Washington, free franking privileges, travel allowances, the ability to use the studios of Congress to make radio and television tapes, and so on. A thousand and one means for keeping his name before the public are put at the disposal of the congressman. It seems to me that no commission and no law could easily attach a value to these things so that their importance to the incumbent would be compensated for by a lower limit on campaign spending during the actual campaign year.

RICHARD M. SCAMMON, director, Elections Research Center of the Governmental Affairs Institute: We hear a great deal of talk in this country about how limited British campaign spending is, and it's true that in Britain expenses are limited during the three weeks of the campaign. But during the previous four years—208 weeks, if my arithmetic is correct—there is no limitation at all. The parties can go out and spend any amounts they want on general party-oriented material.

Quite frankly, I'm more concerned with providing a floor than with limitations on the top. Because if you're going to limit money, are you also, for example, going to eliminate volunteers? Let's say a candidate can get 100 volunteers to man his telephones instead of having to hire them, so that when he sets up his boiler room for primary day, it doesn't cost him. Now, he's obviously got an advantage. And the incumbent has an advantage—all sorts of advantages.

So what I would like to be concerned with on this whole question is not the ethic of limitation, because I don't think this really is very meaningful, but rather providing a floor for every reasonable candidate—public financing, if you want to call it that—*without* the inhibition on raising money. This inhibition, I think, has been written into almost every one of these proposals that I have come across.

Additionally, it seems to me, spending limitations raise a constitutional question, a very real one. I'm a voter, for example, out in Montgomery County, Maryland, and if I want to join with some of my colleagues in my town to support a candidate who is opposed to high rises in our community, I see no reason why we shouldn't gather together and put in $5 each to buy an ad in the local newspaper that says, "Candidate so-and-so is against high-rise zoning and we're for him and vote for him." And I don't see why I should be hauled off to the pokey for doing what amounts to exercising my rights of free speech—and doing it the only way most citizens can do it.

I'd be much more concerned about the floor than I would about the ceiling, and more concerned about free speech than about limits on spending.

MR. BICKEL: Before we get to that, I want to ask one question, because I agree that the real unease about proposals to limit campaign financing is the question, "Why bother?" I mean, what's wrong that requires us to impose limitations? What's wrong with spending $100 million? Obviously campaign money doesn't, in itself, lead to corruption. You can be as corrupt with a ceiling of $21 million as with a ceiling of $35 million. So I just wondered, what is it?

Now, there is a sense abroad—and I'd like both you and Aaron to comment on this—that people buy elections. Wealth is unevenly distributed, and some believe that what is wrong is that if you are a Rockefeller and have your own money—or if you have access to large money, perhaps because of stands you take on issues—you can buy an election. We hear that charge all of the time, of course. It was made against the Kennedys, and it was made against Rockefeller.

How much difference does money make? If a fellow spends $10 million more than the other guy, does he buy himself the election?

MR. SCAMMON: You can't put it on a chart. Obviously, a candidate needs money. If I were going to run for office, I'd like some money to run with. The question is, how much? In other words, can you guarantee that for every increment of one million dollars, you're going to get X-hundred thousand votes? The answer, of course, is obviously you can't. There are too many wealthy men who have tried it and gotten knocked off in primaries or in general elections—including candidate Nelson Rockefeller, who has been trying for a long time with a lot of money.

Money is important, but a successful campaign needs five things: a good man, a good issue, a good organization, good money, and good luck. Of course, if you had all five you couldn't lose. If you didn't have any of the five, you'd be sure to lose.

I don't think one can gainsay that money is important. But, as I suggest, I think it's really more important to put a floor under the legitimate candidate and give him enough so he can make himself heard than it is to give way to this —I don't know what it is really—let's call it this "Puritan ethic," the sense that anybody who spends a lot of money on anything is presumptively immoral.

MR. BICKEL: Yes. I think there's a sense of a sort of monstrously disproportionate allocation of resources, and people start to doubt the fellow's motives in seeking public office. If he is out there pouring money out, what's he after?

MR. SCAMMON: Many times people will wonder why a person is spending $50,000 for a job that only pays $7,500 —in a state legislature, for example.

MR. BICKEL: They are strong feelings, but not strong enough to overcome constitutional doubts, I think. Aaron?

AARON B. WILDAVSKY, dean, Graduate School of Public Policy, University of California at Berkeley: Probably money is most important at the nomination stage. I think it can be said that there is no reasonably well-informed person who thinks that any presidential election in this century would have turned out differently if one or another candidate had more or less money. Indeed, as the Watergate business reveals, having too much money is sometimes as bad as not having enough.

Now, at the nominating stage, of course, there are candidates who drop out because they can't raise the money. In some cases, this is probably good, because it means they don't have the necessary support. In other cases, however, it could be bad if the electorate ends up being deprived of a candidate whose general views might appeal to them but who could not raise the money. I suspect that if one doesn't ask whether Joe Blow or Judy Brown was forced out, but asks instead whether candidates whose views are somewhat in tune with those of the electorate get nominated in spite of a lack of money, the chances are that most political tendencies that could be imagined to have support in the electorate do get some sort of money.

Nevertheless, it is quite possible that we've missed something and that the political process is skewed at the nominating stage. The trouble here is that the difficulties of supporting parties through the public purse mount enormously when you try to do it at the nominating stage, because you don't want to pay people who shouldn't be running anywhere a lot of money so they can bring their nonsense to the attention of the public.

But I must say that I would not talk about this at all, and I think the fact that this issue was raised and has prominence is a symptom of just enormous perversity. What we should be doing is trying to strengthen our parties in this country and not weaken them. If you ask which of our political institutions did well and which did badly, as revealed by Watergate, it's pretty clear. The courts have come out all right, and Congress in its own way has dredged up a lot of information. The press has certainly done its part. But the parties are really a massive failure.

I mean, to me, Watergate isn't interesting so much because somebody did something underhanded—original sin is not a new doctrine—or even because somebody sought to cover up something embarrassing—cover-ups aren't new either. What is really astounding is that the President of the United States has been allowed to persevere in an idiotic course of policy, destructive to the country, destructive to the party, and ultimately destructive to himself.

Now, my understanding is that there was a time in this country when the Henry Cabot Lodges of the world —when there were party bosses in cities, party chairmen in states, and important senators and representatives in Congress who would have descended on the President en masse once they saw he was destroying their party. That is, there were people who had an interest in what party meant, who thought it signified more than just one presidency, and they could have gone to the President and after the first two or three visits would have said, "We are going to denounce you." If Watergate had occurred in the days of centralized bureaucracy in the House of Representatives running from the speaker, the speaker would have said, "We are going to impeach you, if you don't change your behavior." At least the leaders could have gotten him to tell them all of the truth that anybody would want to know and then they would have decided what facts to make public rather than leaving it to him personally.

But if you ask whether this country is prepared to do any of the things we would have to do to have strong parties, I think the answer is no. We are decentralizing the House of Representatives instead of centralizing it— that is, nobody is willing to cut down the merit system and bring back patronage. And nobody, or very few except myself as far as I can tell, is willing to reduce the number of primaries and do other things needed to institute more centralized control. I can't think of any country worth knowing about where political parties are as weak as they are here, or where party leaders are as weak or where it is worth so little of an intelligent and decent person's time to get anywhere in a party.

It seems it's just fundamentally wrong to devise new mechanisms for trying to make people other than party leaders and party members responsible for parties. If we're not willing to strengthen the party system, which has been the extra-constitutional mechanism that has worked to some extent to keep a long-run view going, are we willing to do anything else to bring restraint on our political leaders?

14

MR. BICKEL: Aaron, I take it that public financing is obviously destructive of parties. Does the point go to limitation on expenditures as well?

MR. WILDAVSKY: I don't think that limitations will be too harmful, except in one respect—which is that they are most likely to be out-of-touch with the times, because people will probably be unrealistic or circumstances will probably change. Then—well, you've got to do something and there's a law that says you can't but you absolutely have to do it, then you're going to engage in illicit activity.

MR. WILSON. Could I just add one codicil to what Aaron Wildavsky has said? I agree with everything except one trivial point, but I do want to clarify it because I think it represents a general misperception—not just Aaron's.

I don't think that what we've seen by way of dirty tricks and corrupt and illegal behavior in campaigns is a result of having too much money or too little money or the right amount of money. If Mr. Liddy had been asked to bug the Democratic National Committee's headquarters by a campaign organization that had only a tenth the amount of money that Nixon's had, I think he would still have done it and only charged a tenth as much. It's like the salary paid to the star of a popular television program. That salary isn't determined by the amount of money necessary to get him; it's determined by the amount of money you happen to have—what you can sell the program to the advertiser for.

In fact, I know of very few important decisions in campaign organizations that are made on monetary grounds primarily. Most campaigns do the same thing—and they do more or less of it depending on how much money they have.

However, I do know of decisions made in party organizations, as opposed to campaign organizations, that are made on the basis of money. The need there is to raise the money to keep a permanent cadre of persons employed for party business. Money used for that purpose, it seems to me, is a way of strengthening parties and giving many people a stake in the rightness or wrongness—or, more accurately, in the prudence or imprudence—of the decisions of those who are visible. But the amount of money at the disposal of the Committee to Elect X or Y is, within broad ranges, a relatively unimportant consideration.

MR. WILDAVSKY: I can even remember a time when we were told that if universities and schools accepted federal aid, it wouldn't mean that the Department of Health, Education and Welfare was going to try to tell them whom to hire or fire, what kind of research to do, how to treat people in research programs, or anything like that. The point is that if the public is going to contribute its tax money, then it's going to want to further regulate political parties.

MR. BICKEL: Well, we're into the issue of public financing, obviously. There are other problems. Ralph, I wish you would touch on the legal problems, because they are terribly tough and, again, probably decisive in themselves.

MR. WINTER: Well, public financing, I would suppose, is at its worst when it is combined with the kind of limitations on total expenditures that we're talking about. I say it's at its worst because the natural incentive of incumbents to keep low limits can, in that situation, be combined with the quite attractive campaign pitch that we're helping the taxpayer by not providing much public financing. Indeed, the public financing bills now before the Congress provide terribly little financing.

And one other rather cute little thing: The financing would depend on appropriations before every election, so that nonincumbent candidates would be in the position of waiting for their opposition to appropriate the money, not knowing whether they're supposed to collect money or not collect money. But I suppose we shouldn't let a little thing like that stand in the way of reform.

Let me raise some issues that go to what is the more difficult problem, which is public financing without limitations on expenditures. These, I think, divide really into four groups.

One is the problem of eligibility. As Aaron Wildavsky has mentioned, if you make everyone eligible for public financing, everyone will run. That is, everyone will run except those who have the well-paid job of campaign manager. So you have to have some kind of limitation on who is eligible and most of the formulae, as far as I can determine, seem to make eligible for public financing those candidates who have some kind of relatively widespread support out in the community—which, in most cases, are those candidates who don't need public financing.

MR. BICKEL: Well, on that point, Ralph, there is the problem of measuring the support by the performance in the last election—

MR. WINTER: That's right.

MR. BICKEL: —which seems to me a serious constitutional problem and a major policy problem because it sort of freezes things. I mean, it would have allowed Henry Wallace to run a second time but not the first, and George Wallace to run all of the time because he started early. That's preposterous.

MR. SCAMMON: And it doesn't deal with the question of primary support at all.

MR. BICKEL: And doesn't raise—you know, it's bad policy and very dubious law. On the other hand, if you go to the petition system or something like it for getting on the ballot, oh, boy, you could raise 5 percent or 10 percent of signatures on a vegetarian ticket. Five percent of the American people would come out for anything.

MR. SCAMMON: The money could be enough to make it worthwhile for the solicitors to get the signatures in the first place. So you raise the money to get the signatures so that you can get the money to compensate the people who raise the money.

17

MR. BICKEL: Of course, but it's an excellent investment.

MR. WILDAVSKY: I think there might be a device that would perform the function that has now to be performed in the light of recent events—namely, to reassure the public. People are concerned that unknown, vicious special interests are contributing money and thereby getting special advantage. Also some people are reluctant to contribute to candidates because they're afraid they'll be smeared.

Suppose we had a public mechanism, like a kind of general campaign office, whose sole functions were to rule on the legality of contributions and to publicize them. The basic rule would be that no candidate or any committee in his behalf could spend money on radio or television or newspapers or mail services—where I take it our big expenditures are—directly, with cash. Money for that kind of expenditure would go to the general campaign office, which would give the committee a chit and only with this chit could the committee buy time or deal with newspapers and mailers. The use of cash for these purposes would be forbidden. At the end of the campaign this general campaign office would also make a statement on how much the candidates spent.

Now, what this would do would be to give a reasonable guarantee that, at least, the big money was accounted for, because there would be no point in contributing large sums of money that didn't go for these kinds of purposes. It wouldn't be left to the candidate to reveal the contributions made to him—not many would believe him anyway—and so we might get a little more confidence in what is going on.

My concern with this approach is, of course, that once you establish a little federal office, people will want to do more. And I probably don't want it to do any of the other things they are about to think of.

MR. BICKEL: Well, that's more on the disclosure side, although it could, I suppose, still these inchoate fears about the size of contributions.

Ralph, some of us interrupted you.

MR. WINTER: That's all right, Alex. You know how tolerant I am.

In adjusting these eligibility formulae before every election, it would be very easy to discriminate. It's very much like the question of when will the primary date be held: There are all kinds of incumbent officeholders now who say, "Gee, campaigns are too long. Let's hold the primary a week or two before the general election, save the public money," and all of that. The same kind of thing could go on in adjusting these formulae.

There is also the question of the effect of public financing of campaigns on parties, which is something I find very difficult to fathom. It's total speculation to try and guess what would happen to our parties and to the strength of our parties if we passed these schemes.

Finally, fourth, an issue which seems attractive only to me and the President, the issue of government coercion in matters of conscience. This can be raised, and I've tried to raise it with noticeable lack of success, as a constitutional issue.

I have difficulty with the proposition that the government can go to people and take their money and use it to support ideological causes to which they are indifferent or which they abhor. I realize that we live in a society in which government coerces people to do an awful lot of things. But when it comes to religion we respect this point of conscience. And when it comes to the draft and people having conscientious scruples about war, we respect it. I would really hope that in a society like ours we might also respect conscience when it comes to one's political beliefs. It seems to me to reduce political beliefs to an insignificant level, to a demeaning level, to say that someone can be coerced to support that which he does not believe.

MR. BICKEL: Could the party problem answer at all to a system of regular grants by the government? Everybody would say that, constitutionally, parties are state action anyway; they are governmental instruments.

Suppose there was a system of regular grants for the maintenance of party structures. Again you run into the problem of minor parties, but it's not as difficult as with candidates, because there are bound to be fewer of them. You can define what a party is; somebody has to go through the process of organizing himself as a party and if he does, you give him some money. It's less dangerous than giving money to candidates, because he's not out there hogging the TV lens. Would that meet the problem of the weakness of the party organization at all? At least it would meet Mr. Wilson's problem.

MR. SCAMMON: I doubt very much that the party is weak in America today because it doesn't have a million dollars to spend.

The party is weak in America for a vast variety of reasons: a nonparliamentary system where the whip doesn't mean anything, party ideologies that are fractionalized from Bella Abzug to Biaggi and halfway back, and so on. Really, our colleague David Broder did the book, *The Party's Over,* and I think he probably gave as good a description as any. Greenback infusions — unless you change so many of the other rules of the game—would not by themselves, I think, make a good deal of difference.

MR. BICKEL: Well, then, I'm a little let down, although I'm not startled by the general negativism of the discussion, because I share it.

But before we leave this subject, I do want to raise one question: Is there something that we could do—aside from public financing of campaigns and aside from limitation of expenditures and aside from disclosure, which I think we agree is a separate problem—to increase participation by the people at large in the financing of campaigns? What about tax credits or tax deductions? How could we induce the contribution of gifts on a wide basis? We know it's possible because McGovern did it. And wouldn't that be a good thing for the system?

MR. SCAMMON: Well, you could certainly do it. For example, let's take the easiest approach of all. Suppose you say to the taxpayer, "Work up your tax. You owe the federal government $970. Now you and your wife can give $20 of that to any political group or candidate you want." I think maybe people might give the $20 just to avoid giving it to the federal government—$950 to Uncle and $20 to the National Rifle Association Political Committee or the Anti-National Rifle Association Political Committee or the abortionists or the Right-to-Life group or Candidate X or Y or Z or Alderman Sweeney, or whatever it might be under whatever limitations you wanted to put on it.

This would undoubtedly increase the amount of money infused into the political system. But here comes the major question: What would we get from putting more money into the political system? I mean, would we get less corrupt politics?

MR. BICKEL: No, but we would meet all of the problems that are at all troublesome that public financing would meet.

MR. SCAMMON: Not necessarily, because there is no guarantee that the individual would give this money to the kind of people that we think ought to be assisted by public finance.

MR. BICKEL: But we would make it more possible for the fellow who now has difficulty in penetrating the process to get in, just as public financing would.

MR. WINTER: How?

MR. BICKEL: Because there'd be an incentive so that if he has any support it would be easier for him to raise money. I mean, suppose a candidate has trouble raising seed money. If there were a tax break of this sort, his chances of raising it ought to be doubled.

MR. SCAMMON: They would be certainly increased.

MR. BICKEL: And if the one argument that could be made for public financing is that it would pry open the system at points at which it is undesirably closed, then so would this.

21

MR. SCAMMON: Well, that certainly would do it.

I think here it is important for us to recognize the overconcern of Americans with money in politics. As I've said, money is important in politics, but it is only one of a number of things that are important. However, as long as people are as concerned as they are about money in politics, if this would be an answer, fine. I mean, this would help.

MR. BICKEL: Jim?

MR. WILSON: I want to defend the public horror over some aspects of campaign financing. A large segment of the public, I believe, genuinely thinks that campaign financing as now practiced is corrupt—that is, thinks large amounts of money are raised from groups and corporations and unions in exchange for favors. Now, it's hard to prove this, but people believe it.

And I happen to think they're right in the limited sense that we do have a series of public campaign finance laws on the books today. These are better known as economic regulatory laws. We pass an oil import quota law or a depletion allowance law, or we set up the Civil Aeronautics Board to decide who can fly an airplane from one city to another, or the Interstate Commerce Commission to decide what a trucker can charge on a route from Chicago to Peoria, or the Federal Communications Commission to decide whether or not a station can broadcast and on what frequency and what locations and whether it can also own a newspaper. Whenever we do these things, we give low-visibility government officials enormous discretionary power over important segments of the economy. I don't see why it should be surprising that the list of corporations which have given enormous and often illegal sums of money to the government tends to be headed by the airlines, the oil companies, the broadcast companies, the milk producers. These industries are regulated or subsidized or both.

Now, no one *has* to believe that in exchange for campaign contributions people in government make decisions that nakedly and clearly favor the big giver, because most people who give this money give it to both parties so it kind of cancels it out. Milk producers, I'm sure, give money to as many Democrats as Republicans. But the public sees this as an elaborate, though not very efficient, shakedown. I suspect the people who are giving the money also see it as an elaborate and not very efficient shakedown.

It is pointless to talk about campaign finance reform and about eliminating the incentives for real or imagined corruption without talking about the powerful incentive that exists *now*, built into our system of regulation. Through hints and indirection, through the subtle messages of a Mr. Kalmbach and his equivalents on the Democratic side, a person gets the feeling that he must give money in order to guarantee that his vital interests will not suffer harm. That's where the money comes from, except for those people who, for ideological, personal or friendship reasons, happen to give large amounts of money.

MR. BICKEL: That really leads to limitations on giving. Limits on campaign expenditures wouldn't touch this problem, nor would public financing if you also allowed the candidate to raise additional money or to have the option of raising it. But the problem would be directly met by limitations on giving, which is really the history of our election reforms.

MR. WILDAVSKY: No, it would not. If I understand Jim correctly, what we would have to do is alter the incentive by getting the government out of this endless business of regulation which, on the one hand, does not achieve its direct purpose and, on the other, creates a need among the regulated to influence governmental policy.

MR. BICKEL: That's the radical solution.

MR. SCAMMON: But let's be realistic. We're not going to do that. I think the point that you made, Aaron, about the possibility in some way of assuring total publicity is more realistic.

23

MR. BICKEL: I couldn't agree more. It is an article of faith that somehow the party and the candidate are beholden to the people who put up the money and there are enough instances of fact in this to make one at least think there's a great deal of fire where the smoke exists. But how do you get away from it?

MR. WINTER: But changing the system isn't going to change that. I mean—

MR. SCAMMON: Yes, it will. I would suggest it would.

MR. WINTER: No, take the Agnew example. Mr. Agnew and the supporters of campaign reform have both said, "Look at the Agnew case for an example of something our bills would change." But the fact of the matter is that Mr. Agnew, when he was governor of Maryland and when he was county executive, had discretionary power to reward people through various kinds of regulation. He took money for personal use. The state of Maryland could have had every reform now proposed and Mr. Agnew still would have taken the money, and others still would have given it to him.

MR. BICKEL: Yes, but that's an argument that proves too much.

MR. SCAMMON: That's right, exactly.

MR. BICKEL: It says that no matter what reform or what law we put on the books, it will be breakable.

MR. WINTER: No, it just says that if you have incentives for corruption, the corruption will continue in different forms. That's all it says.

MR. BICKEL: That's correct.

MR. WINTER: And that doesn't prove too much.

MR. BICKEL: That will always be true.

MR. WILDAVSKY: Why don't you pass two laws? The first is the law against venality—

MR. BICKEL: Nobody shall be corrupt.

MR. WILDAVSKY: Yes, and the second is the one they usually advocate in Latin America—the law that says that all of the other laws should be enforced. [Laughter.]

MR. BICKEL: Law number one: corruption is outlawed as of the effective date of this statute. And law number two: all laws are to be enforced impartially as of effective date of this statute.

Well, that would certainly help. It's an appeal to conscience.

MR. SCAMMON: That dismisses it pretty quickly.

MR. WILSON: I'm unwilling to concede for a moment the point that reducing discretionary power in regulated and subsidized industries is impossible or cannot happen.

MR. BICKEL: Well, it's the scenic route.

MR. WILSON: It seems to be that one of the many tragedies and ironies of Watergate is that all of the shoddy deals and all of the nefarious tricks that took advantage of the regulatory climate were perpetrated by an administration, many parts of which were trying slowly to deregulate or to reduce discretionary authority over the broadcast industry and the securities industry, so that people would not be bound by a system which they could not control nor by which the public would be served. And I think that process can be put back on track to some degree. I am not an optimist about anything and least of all about this, I suppose, but I don't think we should give up on it. Or at least we should not say, "Because this is difficult we will invest all of our emotional energies in figuring out ways for people who sign checks to candidates to have those checks photostated and put on the front page of the *New York Times*." I think that's a much less important thing to do.

MR. WINTER: It would improve the front page of the *Times*.

MR. BICKEL: But what are the real objections to this?

MR. HYNEMAN: Might I say a word about alternatives to public financing and the possibility of attracting the American people to contribute to the support of the political parties and candidates?

MR. BICKEL: Sure.

MR. HYNEMAN: First, as to public financing—or rather I should say the use of the income tax system for channeling funds to candidates. This seems to me very unsatisfactory for two reasons: In the first place, it comes once a year, and it comes before we become politically active. You wouldn't be able to express your interest through the income tax after April 15. So this seems to me a very limited device.
   The second thing is that—

MR. BICKEL: You can deduct it next April 15.

MR. HYNEMAN: You can do it a year later, after the campaign is all over.

MR. BICKEL: No. You can deduct it on the April 15th on which you pay your taxes for the previous year.

MR. SCAMMON: Give them the $20 in October and deduct it the following April 15 when you submit your return.

MR. HYNEMAN: Well, okay. I'm not sure the point is flattened, but knock down my second one—which is that only a limited part of the population files an income tax return. By using the income tax system, we would not in any way be attracting support for the political process from a part of the population that we ought to be especially concerned to get involved. It seems to me that we've not yet really tried to attract the American people to give.

Since I figure we're running short of time here, let me simply make a proposition. Consider the fact that the American people support—I should say, very affluently support—many activities that otherwise we would take care of by taxation. They give to United Funds and to individual charitable institutions. I cannot believe that a population which will support causes of that sort—I think maybe I could even say, luxuriously—I cannot believe they would not support their political system if the appeal were made to them.

Now, it occurs to me that if the federal government would contract, let us say, with public utility companies to pay the administrative costs to insert in the bill every month a simple check-off form and an invitation to add to your utility bill whatever amount you want, $2 or $20, designating to whom that goes—it seems to me this would reach as much of the population as any other formal instrument I know of. I offer that as an illustration, not to recommend it above alternatives but to point out that we have possibilities we have not yet tried for getting the American people to finance their political activities. So I think it is totally premature to rush to public financing.

MR. BICKEL: Well, I certainly agree with that.

To come back to limitations, what is the decisive objection to establishing reasonable limits, maybe $5,000 or so per individual, to forbidding or limiting contributions from corporations and labor unions (but not necessarily other organizations, ad hoc organizations, where people just come together with small contributions) and to tightening the enforcement of that by involving the comptroller general of the United States—as the 1971 act does—and by combining it with publicity? (Incidentally I wouldn't let the publicity go below $150 or $200 contribution.)

Of course such a measure could be evaded. It wouldn't cure the Agnew case. It wouldn't cure everything—no law ever does. If a fellow wanted to violate it, he'd violate it.

But wouldn't it meet what I agree is an enormously serious problem, namely, the widespread public cynicism, the belief that politicians sell government services, whether they do it overtly or by quiet understandings.

What is the objection to that?

MR. WINTER: It might cure the cynicism, but it might do something else to the political process that would be very disruptive. Campaign contributions perform a number of functions which allow people to participate in the political process beyond casting the ballot. The contribution allows them—I quote one of my favorite authors, Alex Bickel, on this—"allows them to register intensely felt views and needs."

MR. BICKEL: $5,000 is pretty intense.

MR. WINTER: Now, for instance, suppose somebody feels strongly about the defense of Israel. If he is only allowed to vote in his particular home district, he may have only a very, very limited say on the issue.

There is a need to let people engage in activities beyond their districts, to register the intensity of their feelings. As far as $5,000 being too much, most of the time the people who make those contributions are functional representatives of people with less money who also feel very intensely about the issue.

MR. BICKEL: Well, that can be met. So the limit is set at $10,000 and it's per candidate and you're not restricted to one—your total contribution can go to several candidates over the country. For example, if you're interested in Israel, you'll want to contribute to all kinds of congressmen. All of that could be left open.

What a limit does is meet the spectacle of a Vesco or somebody dumping $250,000 into one campaign. He may not get anything out of it and yesterday's cross-examination [of Harry L. Sears during the trial of former U.S. Attorney General John N. Mitchell] tends to demonstrate that he didn't, but it's ugly and people don't like it. People think it's ugly.

MR. SCAMMON: And sometimes it *is* ugly.

MR. BICKEL: Well, I assume that when it is really ugly, it will happen anyway, because they'll evade the law.

MR. WINTER: But take the case of an emerging issue that people are beginning to feel deeply about. This seems to me a paradigm case. Candidates holding the minority view on the issue are unlikely a lot of times, particularly at the nominating stage, to be able to raise the kind of substantial funds they might need unless they can find some fairly wealthy person or persons to bankroll them for awhile. It's a seed-money function and it's a perfectly reputable function and a terribly important function in the political process.

Until I am persuaded that most of these large contributors are getting some particular kind of rake-off and that there aren't narrower reforms available, until I'm persuaded of that, I am not going to favor something simply because a bunch of propagandists have convinced people that there is something corrupt there.

That really hasn't been shown, Alex.

MR. WILSON: I think that what Mr. Bickel is saying, in fact, is that he really didn't care for Eugene McCarthy or George McGovern, and that's a perfectly respectable view. If we look at their efforts to get off the ground as unknown candidates with no chance to win, we find they did not get started by raising $5, or even $100 or $200, from a large number of people. They got started by finding a few angels. I happen to know who some of these angels were. One of them just bought the *New Republic*.

MR. BICKEL: Yes.

MR. WILSON: And the angels did not put in $5,000 or $10,000; they put in hundreds of thousands. Now, I didn't vote for the candidates who got visibility because of that, but it seems to me that people who may represent emerging trends of opinion, who are unpopular, who have low visibility, should have an opportunity to go to a wealthy friend or two, if they are so fortunate as to have them, and get them to put up the money. I suspect that anybody who has a reasonable chance of tapping a hidden stream in American opinion—this is a point that Aaron made—is going to find such wealthy friends. He may not know them today, he may not live next door to them, but if he's serious and if there is that hidden stream in opinion, he will find them. If it's not a Martin Peretz, it will be somebody else.

I think that kind of flexibility ought to be there, despite my general belief that, to the fullest extent possible, parties and not television ought to structure the electoral process. Nonetheless, even parties need to be told from time to time who the promising candidates are—and that is going to require cantaloupe money, not just seed money.

MR. BICKEL: I would certainly agree that you can't—I wouldn't dream of imposing limits without also instituting some incentive system so that the McCarthys and the McGoverns, although forbidden from getting seed money from one Martin Peretz, could get it more easily from a large number of people.

Well, I think we've about covered the subject. The negativism of our discussion was relieved here and there by the flash of an ill-considered suggestion. [Laughter.]

W E WILL PROCEED now to the second topic for this evening—that is, the problem of the office of the presidency, if it is a problem, and its function.

We will want to talk about such proposed reforms as restricting a President to a single six-year term and perhaps changing the unitary presidency we now have into a multiple presidency, a committee of several presidents who might divide some of the functions among themselves.

We will also want to discuss certain inherent powers of the presidency that many people feel have tended to derogate from the function and powers of Congress—such as the power to impound funds, which President Nixon has claimed, and of course the whole realm of independent presidential powers over the economy and domestic affairs, although those are usually derived from statute. And finally, we may talk about the President's efforts, again efforts that President Nixon had well under way after the 1972 election, to control the federal bureaucracy and to impose his will upon it, this being a problem that has been recognized as pervasive in many presidencies.

Again, I will begin with Mr. Winter.

MR. WINTER: I think a good place to begin is the question —what is there about Watergate that makes us think that the President has too much power? If you really look at the record and look at Watergate closely, it comes down to two things:

The first is that the people who directed the break-in had access to manpower and technology. It may well be that an administration in power has better access to those things than people who are not in power. Yet I certainly think that we can all agree that the President has no monopoly in that area.

The other source of power that enters into Watergate —and this goes to the problem of campaign financing, particularly the illegal corporate contributions—is the power that Professor Wilson was talking about earlier, the great discretionary power of the executive branch to regulate the economy. The existence of this power creates the temptation to ask for funds and the temptation to contribute them even when it is illegal. Watergate and excessive presidential power are thus only partially related.

In any event much of the rhetoric about presidential power mistakes the sources of that power. The sources of presidential power to some extent lie in foreign affairs and the increased importance of foreign affairs, the fact that the President commands large armed forces, controls the instrumentalities of our intelligence agencies, and the like.

31

But the President also has a large amount of power which Congress has given to him, power over businessmen and unions. He also has power over local politicians by being able to allocate manpower training grants, urban renewal grants, and the like. I think the effect of this has changed the presidency in subtle ways. Increasingly, groups within our society are looking to the presidency as a way of fulfilling their narrow special interests, rather than looking to it in terms of broader issues such as war and peace. I would suspect that businessmen, unions, and local politicians in 1965, approaching President Johnson in the hope of fulfilling their narrow interests, did not, while they were lobbying for those interests, make comments upon his foreign policy. Indeed, I suspect it was quite a while before foreign policy and the war really became an issue to which those groups thought they had to pay any attention.

Now, I don't know what we can do about this. One idea is to stop delegating power to the President. But those in the Congress who seem most disturbed by presidential power also seem most anxious to delegate more. I guess the phrase is, "Hating the dictator but liking the dictatorship."

The way to control presidential power is for Congress to strengthen itself. It ought not shirk responsibility as it did with the war, declaring neither war nor peace. In a way, I think it is fair to say it has relied on the President's impounding of funds so that it could both vote to spend money and not vote to increase taxes.

Separation of powers, it seems to me, really involves two strong branches—leaving the judiciary out—two strong branches each operating within its realm of responsibility, not one branch constantly trying to weaken the other. I conclude, therefore, that we ought not to make radical institutional changes in the presidency. We ought to cease to delegate power to it, and Congress ought to get control of its own affairs, get an institutional sense of its own mission, react to presidential exercises of power out of a sense of the institution and not solely out of a sense of who is helped or who is hurt.

If one goes through the records of the Separation of Powers Subcommittee [of the Senate Judiciary Committee], one finds, for example, that executive orders in the area of civil rights are praised by the same people who condemn executive orders in the area of internal subversion, and vice versa. No particular group in the Congress ever gets together and says, "These executive orders raise a question of presidential intrusion in the congressional domain; we ought to be concerned not about the monetary result but about this kind of exercise of power." We don't see that. Until we do, there's not much we can do about presidential power.

MR. BICKEL: Aaron, you're a student of the presidency.

MR. WILDAVSKY: I've concluded that there are only three things that can be said about Watergate with absolute certainty.

The first is that we will not see a repetition of its like again for the next twenty or twenty-five years because the sanctions it has already imposed are so great that we won't have to guard against it. You know the saying about generals unnecessarily preparing to fight the last war.

The second absolute certainty is that we will once again, yet more, without doubt, want a President who will override a conservative Supreme Court and a recalcitrant Congress. There will come a time when we feel the need is for action and energy and dispatch, and we will not truck any opposition to our then hero.

And I think the third thing, of course, is that Watergate doesn't have any lessons. Watergate is like a Rorschach. If you want to know what anybody thinks is wrong with the country, ask him what Watergate has to teach us. If you want to know what's deep inside of any person, ask what he or she thinks of Watergate, and you will get a response.

I like checks and balances. I like the separation of powers. I like conflicts. Therefore, I want all our institutions to be invigorated. I'd like to see Congress gain more control over its ancient power of the purse, and I'd like to see the courts handle some of their responsibilities in the area of crime more forcefully, and stay out of some of the more political areas which they have invaded, and so on.

But I don't think there's anything you can learn from Watergate. Let me just give a few examples. One lesson that's suggested is that somehow the Senate ought to confirm the appointments of the President's closest advisers. But what Watergate shows us is that the President won't take advice or even see the people he himself has appointed! What would happen? You'd ask for the confirmation of somebody, he'd sit in a little office in the White House, and after six months of no papers arriving at his desk, he would go home.

Another proposal is for the six-year term. I'm opposed to it because, among other things, I don't think Richard Nixon deserves to have an amendment named after him.

What we really have now, to use the lawyers' concept that hard cases make bad law, is an anti-third-term amendment which guarantees that if we ever in our lifetime find a President who is worth keeping in office, we won't be able to keep him. And if we hadn't limited Presidents to two four-year terms, then nobody would have thought of limiting them to one six-year term. The proposal seems to assume that the safety of the country is guaranteed, not by the checks and balances of vigorous institutions, but by taking an electoral check away from the President. After all, as far as we know, Nixon *did* behave somewhat better in his first term, perhaps because he was concerned about reelection. In any event, putting a man in office who never has to run again doesn't guarantee he won't be interested in his successor, and it may make him much less interested in what anybody thinks—a very peculiar doctrine for a democratic country!

How about the proposal for a parliamentary system? The one good thing that came from the recent parliamentary crises in Britain and Israel is that they indicated that any system has its defects. As we watched while these countries failed to get a government for some period of time, we understood that parliamentary government isn't all a bed of roses.

The point I would stress here is that parliamentary government is preeminently party government. It requires an electorate that will put in office either a majority party or a compatible coalition, and it requires political parties that will vigorously control their membership in the legislature. Why a country that won't do anything to strengthen its political parties, that spends all its time thinking of ways to weaken them, would ever contemplate adopting a parliamentary regime, I cannot imagine.

So, what I think we basically have seen are exercises in foolishness.

On the other hand, I think that Watergate is a mechanism for coming to grips with one's self. If you forget about the pulling and the hauling, it raises for us the question of what kind of country we want, what kind of people we are, and what kind of institutions fit us best. In this respect, I see the one cheerful prospect. I have noticed that the words of the Founding Fathers are once again in fashion—and that the words of our Constitution are simply not a way of putting down unfortunate minorities, but have achieved a renewed nobility. Perhaps that is at least one gain that we can count from this.

MR. BICKEL: One silly reform that you didn't bother to mention, and that I did mention in my introductory remarks, is this idea of a committee presidency. It reminds me of nothing so much as the decline and fall of the Roman Empire, which is attributed, in part, to the creation by Diocletian of two emperors and two Caesars to rule. If we had a multiple presidency, the incumbents would fight each other like lions in a cage, wouldn't they?

MR. WILDAVSKY: At least now we can have some small catharsis because we know whom to blame.

MR. WILSON: I would like to point out for the record, Mr. Bickel, that the decisive speech in the Constitutional Convention in opposition to the committee concept of the presidency was delivered by James Wilson. His judgment has been confirmed amply ever since.

MR. BICKEL: A fine lawyer he was.

MR. WINTER: It is a good example of how bizarre proposals get, because the most recent proposal for the committee presidency was for an even number so there wouldn't even be a way to break ties.

MR. WILDAVSKY: Certainly, they will achieve their object. Presidents will be unable to do any harm at all, and they will also be unable to do any good. That's a fair trade?

MR. BICKEL: I want to take up one point that you made, Aaron. This President has felt—as have other Presidents, and I think justly so—that he comes into office, he's got the mandate, and he can't get a grip on the bureaucracy. He sends his solicitor general or attorney general into the Supreme Court to argue one position on busing or what have you but, at the lower level, the bureaucracy in the district courts or the bureaucracy of HEW dealing with school districts follows a different policy. And he can't come to grips with it.

This problem isn't novel with Mr. Nixon. But he tried to solve it in a way that I do think raises problems in a democratic society, namely, by fanning out of the White House faceless people who would undermine visible and accountable cabinet officers, by trying to control in that fashion.

Now, sure, it's silly to ask that the President's domestic affairs assistant be confirmed by the Senate, but it is not for nothing that the Constitution contemplates great departments of government headed by men who are confirmed by the Senate. It isn't silly to insist, especially in a government this large, that there be visibility and accountability under the President. Everybody understands he can't do everything himself, but what is done in his name ought to be done visibly by people who in some fashion are accountable and in some sense have a connection with the country. It's a lot better for Kissinger to be secretary of state than even for Kissinger to be operating out of the White House.

MR. SCAMMON: Alex, as you know, I was a bureaucrat for four years in the Commerce Department, and I must say that your point makes so much sense. In the bureaucracy as I knew it under President Kennedy—and I think it is true under Nixon and everybody else—sure there might be some who would try deliberately to sabotage, but not many. And if they did, they would be eliminated.

The fact is that most bureaucrats want to do what they are supposed to do—particularly if there is a clear leadership and a clear distinction between the political and the administrative function, if there isn't a lot of shilly-shallying about the policy. If they know what the policy is and what the course is that we are going to follow, the great majority will follow it.

I must say I never found that this was a difficult problem, either in the State Department where I served for seven years or in Commerce where I served for four. Now, admittedly, these were Democratic administrations, and they may be different from Republican administrations. But I don't really think so, except that with our Republican friends I think there has been a tendency in the past to bring in people who themselves begin with the premise that the bureaucrat is out there to disembowel them at the earliest opportunity, which just isn't the case.

MR. BICKEL: But, Dick, Harry Truman complained that he couldn't control the State Department. And John F. Kennedy complained that he couldn't impose his will on the State Department.

MR. SCAMMON: Yes, but you're dealing with a very special case here of foreign affairs in the State Department. I am talking about the bureaucracy generally—the Veterans Administration, HEW, and so on.

MR. BICKEL: Under Nixon they virtually went into civil disobedience against the secretary.

MR. SCAMMON: Yes, but if the Nixon people had really put it on the basis of who was in charge, I think they would have won.

MR. WILSON: Alex, I think that the problem of bureaucracy is great and that the President is right to be deeply concerned about it. But the problem is typically misconceived either as willful men attempting to subvert the President or as twenty years of Democratic appointees in the bureaucracy leaving a Republican President helpless. I don't think either one of those explanations really covers bureaucratic behavior.

HEW is a good example of the more accurate explanation. HEW is not a bureau. It is a conglomerate. It is the ITT of government. Every bureau one can imagine whose affairs may touch humanity, large or small, can find a niche under this huge umbrella. And those bureaus have specially defined missions set up by different Congresses to serve different publics—to make the schools richer or smaller or better or blacker or whiter, and the same with welfare, social services, and vocational rehabilitation. They work at cross purposes because they were set at cross purposes by the Congress. And the problem of the President is to preside over an agency—or the problem of the secretary of HEW is to preside over an agency—in which, without the ability to repeal some purposes and put new purposes into effect, he must tolerate the constant guerrilla warfare carried on by men and women who are good-spirited, good-intentioned, and trying to do their jobs.

Again, it seems to me much like the problem of economic regulation. We may not get the government we deserve, but we tend to get the government we want. We tend to get those things done that we have asked Congress to do. When Congress does it, it creates a bureau and the bureau acquires a life of its own. There's no way to deal with that simply by means of various strategies of staffing the higher levels of government.

I do agree with you, however, that the cabinet head is a much maligned individual, and that the maligning started not with Mr. Nixon, but with Mr. Kennedy and Mr. Johnson, because they thought the government could be run by a small group of persons in the West Wing of the White House. It cannot be.

Some critics, without acknowledging their earlier error, are now changing their minds. Mr. Arthur Schlesinger in 1963, after celebrating the end of Camelot, complained that the State Department was an inefficient, incompetent, backward bureaucracy that every President should ignore. Now ten years later, in *The Imperial Presidency*, he belabors the President for overlooking the accumulated wisdom, expertise, and statesmanship of our established branches of government. I think this sort of thing really ought not to be tolerated in public rhetoric.

MR. BICKEL: I don't disagree with your diagnosis of the problem or with Dick's, and you know infinitely more about it than I do. But there is, I think, a psychological strain that connects with Watergate—and that has to do with the way the Nixon White House went at it.

MR. WILDAVSKY: Alex, let's see if we can't distinguish what Nixon did from what other Presidents have done. With Nixon, we have a President who tried to run a foreign policy without the Senate, an expenditure policy without the House, a national campaign without his party, a government against the bureaucracy—and even, we now learn, was against big business on whom the arm was put times too numerous to mention.

So it seems that Nixon has essentially a Gaullist or plebiscitary view: "I'm the people; you are nothing. If you pass a bill over my veto to spend, I still won't spend because I'm in touch with all of the people, and you are narrow and parochial and so forth." We see, in the Nixon presidency, I think, a kind of a medical museum case of immediate, direct contact between the President and the unwashed masses, with no intermediary institutions such as those that are carefully enumerated in our Constitution.

MR. HYNEMAN: Maybe we ought to import another population to elect the President.

MR. WILDAVSKY: I'd like to expand a bit on Jim's point, because there are continuities from at least Kennedy through Nixon.

One of these is that increasingly we have taken on social programs where we understand the inputs, namely the money, but we don't understand the outputs at all. So there's frustration that gets blamed on the bureaucracy. Eventually, we are going to have more than half the country working in the bureaucracy, and then they will blame themselves. It's an inevitable development.

To be specific, if we don't know how to have an educational program that will rapidly improve the cognitive and reading abilities of poor and deprived children, then bureaucracies are the scapegoat for the failure. And the same is true for the innumerable other poverty programs. The first thing we do is to set impossible standards. And the second thing we do is to blame the bureaucracy for not achieving them.

A second line of continuity—this was especially blatant in the Kennedy administration (just read Schlesinger's book and the others by the staff members)—is that the top officials don't contemplate checks and balances. To them separation of powers is an anathema. "We have wonderful ideas that are sabotaged out there. If only there were cooperation, social policy would be much better."

This view, I think, is completely false. Actually, it ignores the notion that, on occasion, people in the bureaucracy are supposed to oppose the President—in part because they are supposed to pay attention to other branches of government, like the courts and Congress, and in part because they have clientele groups on whom they are dependent and who depend on them, and it has become an informal norm that to some degree they represent these groups. In fact, it would not normally be thought to be a good idea for a President to have a secretary of agriculture who was hated by all the farmers, a secretary of the interior hated by all the conservationists, and a secretary of labor hated by the union people.

MR. BICKEL: You're describing the present situation.

MR. WILDAVSKY: Yes, but I point out to you that the present situation is an intensification of past trends. I think the seeds for this were apparent in the Kennedy and Johnson administrations—in the sense of acting in terms of a peculiar doctrine about the bureaucracy, one that holds it responsible for not understanding public policy and fails to recognize separation of powers and checks and balances as these principles affect the bureaucracy. What Nixon has done with his special problems and personalities is kind of to give us an overview of what this doctrine would look like if it were, in fact, put into practice.

MR. BICKEL: The point that I was reaching for is very much connected to yours. Indeed some of the things you said earlier about the plebiscitary presidency, and so forth, I was going to say in almost the same words. It seems to me—of course, this is a trend that has been going on— that the Nixon administration after the election, with the reorganization plans it had, the fanning of these people out of the White House, the super-cabinet—that all of this was a scheme for trying to control the bureaucracy, for trying to get more unity into the administration. It was a scheme to destroy the institutional company of the President.

Presidents in the past, no matter how powerful and how active and how popular and plebiscitary they regarded themselves, have acted within an "executive company" made up of heads of departments, people with constituencies of their own—not bureaucracy, but people of some standing as heads of departments. If F. D. R. didn't like what Jesse Jones was doing, he had to negotiate with him because Jesse Jones was a power of some sort.

Now, the Nixon scheme was to control out of the White House—to have faceless men in cabinet offices and

41

to de-institutionalize the immediate surroundings of the President. And that, I must say, seems to me to connect with a psychology that can lead to a Watergate: the plebiscitary notion that the election of the President is the conclusion, the culmination, and the end of a political process until the next election.

MR. SCAMMON: I think, Alex, we really have to go back to what Jim said before—and this applies to Nixon and to the Johnson administration and the Kennedy administration and, to some extent, to the Truman administration. As government becomes more the Goliath, we expect it to do so much more than we ever did even during the depression. We expect it to regulate this, regulate that, solve this, solve that, make horse harnesses fit for every type of horse, do this, do that, provide instant answers and, besides, get the answer in yesterday.

We expect all these things. Many political leaders on both sides of the aisle in Congress and many searchers after presidential nominations are prepared to promise so much. For example, look at some of the discussions on health insurance that are going on now, both in and out of the government, involving both those who are proposing plans in the Senate and those supporting the President's proposal. The promises that are being made, the hopes that are being held out, are so enormous that I think Aaron's estimate about half the population ending up in the bureaucracy would have to be viewed as a minimum.

The fact is that if you see government as the answer man, if you see government as the supplier, if you see government as the fount, you are obviously going to have a lot of the troubles that Professor Schlesinger has described in his *Imperial Presidency*. And I just don't know how we are going to beat this. I don't know really how we are going to avoid in the long run a cycle of promise and frustration leading eventually to the hero figure who, as Aaron quite properly points out, comes in because he can cut the Gordian knot. He becomes the hero man, and then we change the Constitution and reelect him eight times.

42

MR. WINTER: It is very interesting you say this. You talk about the frustration, because almost all of the calls for reform that we have heard after Watergate, we were hearing with only a little less intensity before Watergate, and from the same people.

These calls follow the Great Society. And they are a result, I think, of the frustration over the failure of the Great Society, the unwillingness of the advocates of the Great Society to admit that it failed, so instead they search around to find somebody to point their finger at. Right now the culprit is campaign financing: the fat cats are buying government and that's why government is not working, or the President is too powerful, or something else—

MR. BICKEL: It's the irony that we noted before. Here is an administration which programmatically, philosophically, intended to dismantle, but which, institutionally, did the exact opposite. It carried the aggrandizement of the presidency and the destruction of the companion institutions several steps—really several leagues—past anybody else.

MR. SCAMMON: It seems to me, Alex, that maybe the basic lesson from Watergate, if we learn it at all, is that government *is* going to do these various things we want it to do. I don't think we are going to move backwards on this. With all respect to your view, Jim, I just think it is romantic to assume we are, and I don't think you assume that we are going to change this.

MR. WINTER: You say the only alternative is to move to the great hero.

MR. SCAMMON: No, I think the alternative is to—if I may quote a past President, "Come, let us reason together." In other words, I think the problem really is to establish some kind of norm as to what we can reasonably expect from our institutions—not expect instant answers from them, not expect the bureaucracy to change overnight, not expect anything to come up seven for twenty-eight times in a row, which is really the kind of performance we expect from government today.

MR. BICKEL: So our answers here are more attitudinal and psychological than—

MR. SCAMMON: They may well be.

MR. BICKEL: Thank you very much. I think that concludes this part of our discussion. [Applause.]

# PART II

Alexander M. Bickel, *Chairman*

Richard M. Scammon
Harry H. Wellington
James Q. Wilson
Ralph K. Winter, Jr.

ALEXANDER BICKEL, chairman of the Round Table: This is the second of our two Round Tables on the lessons, if any, to be drawn from the Watergate affair. We will try, as we did last night, not to assume that something must necessarily be done. Reform and change are not self-evidently virtuous aims, and Watergate, although certainly a grave malfunction in the system, may just possibly not have turned up any fundamental defects in it.

Lawbreaking has always been with us and it's a fair guess that it will continue to be. Yet it would be reckless to disregard the fact that Watergate, at the very least, presents an opportunity to reexamine some of our structures and procedures and has created a favorable climate for reforms, whether or not those reforms are necessarily related to whatever the Watergate affair, as such, may have revealed.

The session tonight will deal first with the President's powers and functions in the areas of domestic and national security; then with the problem of politics infringing on the Department of Justice, on the administration of justice, and the possible need for institutionalized special prosecutors; and finally with some matters of immediate concern and interest, such as the reach of the impeachment power, its relationship to claims of executive privilege, and its relationships to and accommodation with the criminal process.

47

**A**S TO THE POWERS of the President to guard domestic security against rebellion, terrorism, and the like, and national security against foreign enemies, the issue is really one of emergency powers which may inhere in the President to wiretap and perhaps otherwise to impinge on normal civil rights. Extreme claims have gone so far as to say that the President may do virtually anything short of ordering executions. Well on this side of such extreme claims, there is an area, a debatable area, of inherent presidential powers.

The centerpiece of our discussion at this Round Table, as at the first one, is the study by Ralph Winter entitled *Watergate and the Law.* And I will therefore call on him to lead us off. Ralph?

MR. WINTER: Thank you, Alex. I don't know that there is a serious problem as to presidential power where domestic security is involved. That is to say, I'm not convinced that the normal operation of the criminal law is not sufficient to protect the nation against whatever dangers there may be—and there certainly is danger in expanding presidential power in the area of domestic security. The principal way of expanding it, really, is to allow all kinds of surveillance and other kinds of activities directed at people the executive branch thinks are merely inclined to break the law.

The President may well have extraordinary powers in the event of a complete breakdown of law. But in the normal situation—all too normal, one might say—of terrorists and the like, there is little evidence that changes in existing law are necessary.

Where national security is concerned, a lot of people think that presidential power is considerably greater. (By national security I mean where there is foreign involvement.) I would think—and I'm prepared to defend the position—that we ought not attempt, through legislation, to restrict the President's power in national security beyond the restrictions that are now applied.

48

There would be several dangers in doing so. One is that any restriction would be very likely to contain ambiguous language which might, in fact, empower the President to do more than he is now empowered to do explicitly—rather like the problem that arises in the war power bills.

A second is that I'm not convinced that the President doesn't need a great deal of flexibility where national security matters are involved. Major governments do engage in various kinds of activities which go beyond normal law enforcement procedures—such as wiretapping of embassies without a warrant.

Another reason that explicit restrictions are unwise is that once we get four years beyond Watergate—perhaps not even that far—these things are going to happen anyway, and a law that attempts to restrict the President too much will be a law that is broken. It will be a law that is not obeyed; we will get in the habit of not obeying it, and we will find that, indeed, what we are really afraid of, the abuse of this power, will begin to happen because the law itself is too unreasonable.

It seems to me that what we ought to do is somehow impose procedures which elevate the threshold at which the executive branch engages in these activities. We have to increase the political sanction for abuses of the power. One way of doing this, I think, is to assign explicitly the responsibility for ordering such acts so that we don't have what appears to have happened in the Watergate affair— a situation in which subordinate members of the executive branch were authorizing things in the name of national security, a situation in which the subordinates may or may not have thought they had authority, a situation in which those higher up may or may not have thought they could disavow what was happening.

It seems to me you increase the threshold at which the executive will do things when you explicitly lodge sole authority for ordering such acts in responsible officials. Where, for example, there's wiretapping because of foreign or military affairs, we should require the signature not only of the attorney general but also of the secretary of defense or secretary of state. In any event we should lodge responsibility explicitly in accountable officials so that abuses aren't encouraged because of confusion as to who has authority to do what.

MR. BICKEL: I might just add by way of clarification that until 1972—am I right?—the law on the subject was wide open and the practice of wiretapping—breaking and entering is quite a different matter—wiretapping had been pursued in domestic security affairs since the administration of Franklin D. Roosevelt. In 1972 the Supreme Court held that that was unconstitutional without a warrant—although Justice Powell, anyway, suggested that the warrant procedures might be a little different than they are in the normal criminal case and that Congress might provide for such warrant procedures.

The question of whether wiretapping on the President's own authority without a warrant in foreign security cases —that is, national security cases, involving foreign embassies and the like—the question of whether that's constitutional without a warrant is an open question. The Court didn't say "no," it didn't say "yes," and the question is open. But I take it that domestic wiretapping without a warrant—which the Nixon administration engaged in as much as prior administrations, perhaps more, perhaps less —I take it that that's stopped.

So there is some law on the subject and there is an opportunity for some statutory intervention if Congress chose to do it. As things now stand, you have to get the same kind of a warrant in a domestic security case as you would in a normal criminal case, which may be a little difficult.

MR. WINTER: But to get the warrant you must show probable cause. The kind of statute that Justice Powell seemed to have been talking about is, I would think, a statute which really authorizes warrants where the particular officer of the government has a subjective belief that certain people are inclined to violate the law. I mean, it's hard for me to see how one relaxes the procedures without getting to that, and I think inclination or belief in inclination is just too flexible.

MR. BICKEL: I'm not advocating that kind of a statute. There'd still be the security of going before a judge, so that the executive officer's subjective impression would have to run the gauntlet of a federal judge's sharing it or not sharing it, of finding that the impression was paranoia or seemed real.

MR. WILSON: There are various forms of surveillance in the area of domestic security that are not electronic in nature—that involve, for example, the infiltration of extremist groups somehow defined, or the surveillance and questioning of their members, developing dossiers and so on. I don't think we should leave this discussion on the implicit assumption that the law in this area is clear.

As near as I can tell, the law in this area is quite ambiguous, if indeed it exists at all. The Federal Bureau of Investigation has held for many years—and not simply under Mr. Nixon—that it was its responsibility to maintain fairly close surveillance over groups it defined as extremist in some sense. Now, if you happen to be a member of an extremist group of the left, you are opposed to this, until it is pointed out to you that surveillance is also taking place with respect to the Ku Klux Klan. And I suppose if you're a member of the Ku Klux Klan, you're opposed until you realize it also takes place with respect to the SDS [Students for a Democratic Society].

I am not a lawyer, a point which I hope to repeat many times this evening, but I don't think that the law is sufficiently clear, nor am I certain in my own mind that we know how to draft a regulation, much less a statute, that would place clear and feasible boundaries around this aspect of investigative authority. I think we ought to acknowledge the ambiguity in this area, because one of the charges that has been leveled at the Nixon administration is that, to an inordinate degree, it encouraged the FBI and other agencies to maintain active surveillance.

MR. BICKEL: I agree. There isn't any law on the subject that I know. There was a case in Chicago involving a man who was being shadowed. The FBI was just following him around, and he went to court to get an injunction against the FBI's doing that.

MR. WILSON: Mr. Giancana, yes.

MR. BICKEL: That's the fellow. The thing ended ambivalently, if memory serves, because it's difficult to find in the Constitution or anywhere a right of privacy against being observed essentially in public places. This applies also to infiltration of groups. I mean, if you're the Klan or the SDS and you freely recruit people, I don't think the Constitution guarantees you that the people you recruit are there in good faith.

It is, I agree, very difficult to imagine the ground rules that would apply to this.

HARRY H. WELLINGTON, professor of law, Yale Law School: We do have them.

MR. BICKEL: And it's very difficult to think of a country that has no power to do this.

MR. WELLINGTON: We do have some law respecting entrapment, for example, which looks in quite a different direction from the law having to do with wiretapping. The government has a very substantial amount of power to infiltrate an organization and to engage in what the layman would think of as entrapment. The Supreme Court in the Russell case—that was 1973, I believe—upheld forms of entrapment.

MR. BICKEL: Well, up to a certain point.

MR. WELLINGTON: But a very substantial point. I was wondering, though—

MR. BICKEL: Perhaps you had better explain entrapment, Harry.

MR. WELLINGTON: I wish I could. [Laughter.]
Entrapment is, typically, infiltrating an organization and, in some fashion or another, inducing someone to commit a crime. It's a fairly technical—

MR. BICKEL: Like a narcotics sale, for example. You suspect a fellow—

MR. WELLINGTON: Yes, but the infiltration could also be into a left- or right-wing group.
I have a great deal of sympathy with Ralph's presentation on the distinction between domestic and foreign security matters. It makes good sense. You can write it out and suggest different laws for domestic and foreign security matters. It's easy at the extremes. But in practice, isn't there a very real difficulty in separating the two? Aren't they very often intertwined?

MR. BICKEL: As in the Ellsberg case, for example, where the claim was that they went out for Ellsberg when they thought that he delivered a set of the Pentagon Papers to the Russians.

MR. WELLINGTON: That's quite right.

MR. WILSON: Or the Venceremos Brigade, a group of domestic persons of an extreme political persuasion who, nonetheless, made a trip to Havana when other Americans had not made the trip. Now, did that fall in the area of domestic security or foreign security, or was it security at all? I have a feeling, as a political scientist, rather than a lawyer—

MR. BICKEL: You're not a lawyer?

MR. WILSON: No, I'm not. [Laughter.]

MR. WELLINGTON: We're not political scientists, by the way. [Laughter.]

MR. WILSON: I feel that, given the Watergate atmosphere, this might not be a very useful time to engage in such legal clarification as might be necessary in this area. It is a time in which the perspective necessary to make these judgments may be lost because of the preoccupation with the real or alleged involvement of the present administration in furthering these activities. I happen to think the problem exists without regard to the present administration, and it might be useful to address the problem at a time when we could abstract from the nature of the incumbent.

MR. WINTER: Well, I think that all of us in this room, being calm types that are not overcome by waves of hysteria, can say a few things, even though none of us is both a political scientist and a lawyer.

It does seem to me that the distinction is shadowy, but that's a good thing—a good reason for not liberalizing the law on the domestic side, for keeping it fairly strong—because that increases the political risks to administrations that take actions in the name of national security that touch on domestic matters. I would not like to see the law clarified to a great degree because clarification might, in fact, reduce the threshold by drawing the line one place rather than another. Instead I'd like to see every administration thinking, "Well, we don't want to wind up in court over this and we will if it's not clearly national security."

That's the kind of a system I would like. I think the whole Watergate incident illustrates this—that the Ellsberg burglary, in fact, was way over on the domestic side, and it was the fact that it did get into court that makes the political risk great.

MR. BICKEL: Well, not only that—it's always nice to find a silver lining in Watergate—but also what Watergate appears to have done, without the need for any law to express it, is to draw a line between, on the one hand, infiltrating, shadowing, entrapping—that is, things that are done by government, by the FBI or what have you, in public so to speak, against activities that are themselves public—and, on the other hand, wiretapping and of course breaking and entering, as in the Ellsberg case. Now we know, with reasonable assurance, that even though J. Edgar Hoover said no to the Tom Charles Huston plan, the FBI itself had in the past engaged in some breaking and entering.

I venture that the bright line between shadowing, entrapping, and infiltrating on the one hand and breaking and entering on the other is pretty clear now—clear to the FBI and clear across the board, whether the case is domestic or foreign. No law is needed, but it is a very good thing for that to have happened.

MR. WELLINGTON: But I meant to be coming at this from the civil libertarian point of view and wondering whether the Supreme Court's decision requiring a warrant in domestic security ought not to be extended to cover foreign security matters. The principal argument against such a rule is the extreme sensitivity of foreign security matters and the risk of involving the courts in them. Yet if the distinction between foreign and domestic is shadowy, if the two areas are intertwined, I wonder whether we might not be able to trust our judges with the foreign as well as the domestic.

MR. BICKEL: But I would imagine, though, that foreign security parcels out into a number of situations. We all keep thinking of it as placing a tap on the Russian embassy and, sure, we can trust Judge Sirica with that. But extend it a little further—think of it as some CIA or intelligence operation, as some Ian Fleming plot or as *The Spy Who Came in from the Cold*, with allies and foreign agents involved and so forth.

There was a case in the fifties—the case of Colonel Abel, the Russian spy, and there's a Supreme Court opinion at great length which forswears any need for warrants. The FBI broke in on him and searched him without a warrant. And the Court says, "Well, that's a foreign matter —it's a different matter."

One does hesitate when the matter is visualized that way—as a real intelligence operation rather than just the tapping of the phones of the Russian embassy. It does become a little "icky" to think of a judge passing on that, being given the facts, and that is, I think, where the hesitation comes. Of course, the question is open.

MR. WELLINGTON: I don't mean to suggest that there is an easy answer. It's a trade-off, and the question is how we ought to err. I'm inclined to think that we ought to err in favor of the individual by requiring a warrant.

It may be, however, that with time and experience we can have a finer distinction than the gross one between foreign and domestic security.

MR. BICKEL: It's certainly possible to require federal agents to come in on national security cases and disclose to the judge, if they can, and if they can't to hand the judge a sealed affidavit indicating the reasons why they can't disclose and asking the judge to issue the warrant on their authority. This is not a wholly unaccustomed thing in the law. There are instances where judicial power is invoked on the authority of the executive without going to trial with that.

MR. WELLINGTON: But irrespective of how one comes out on a warrant, Ralph's suggestions as to who may order a wiretap make good sense. There should be clear responsibility in some high official in addition to the attorney general. The power ought not be in White House people who have staff positions at the pleasure of the President.

MR. BICKEL: Yes, I agree that's a very fruitful suggestion, and I also think we've probably rounded off this topic as best we can.

THE SECOND TOPIC that we're going to discuss this evening relates more immediately to the Watergate experience. It's the problem of political control by the President, by an administration, which can be exercised to influence the Department of Justice in its administration of justice. For example, when it comes to prosecuting close associates of the President himself—as in the current instance, as happened in the Truman administration, as happened in the Teapot Dome case in the 1920s—obviously questions are raised. At the very least, misgivings are legitimately entertained about the administration in effect prosecuting itself.

The key issues are: Should we take the Department of Justice out of the executive department, making it independent in some fashion, not subject to control by the President? Or should we provide ways for appointing special prosecutors who would be entirely free and independent of presidential control—institutionalizing them in some fashion. Ways of doing that might include setting up an independent prosecutor as a permanent office, or providing standby authority for doing it.

These are the issues and, again, I'll start with Ralph who has something to say about them in his report.

MR. WINTER: Well, it's always tempting in the wake of an event like Watergate to contemplate separating the Justice Department from the political branches, to say that the administration of justice must not be affected by partisan considerations. The problem is, of course, that the Justice Department also has very important policy decisions to make. There are decisions about the allocation of resources: Should there be more money in the Law Enforcement Assistance Administration, or more money to prosecute civil rights cases or organized crime, or should the money go into other kinds of litigations? And what cases should be taken to the Supreme Court, what should the government's position be, and various constitutional

57

questions. I would think one would normally want these decisions to be resolved by officials who are accountable to the people through the President, one of the things Presidents ought to run on.

As we get down to particular litigation, the dangers of partisan control are greater and perhaps the need for electoral control is slightly less. I don't mean to say it's not there. But I do think that the need for having someone who is a presidential appointee in every case before the Justice Department is somewhat less, although I strongly feel that as far as settlements and consent decrees and the like are concerned, the basic policies decided upon by the political officers have to be enforced.

It does seem to me, though, that there are a few areas in which special prosecutors and what I call counsels, special counsels to grand juries, would be useful. I don't think the case for a permanent special prosecutor has been made. But I think there is a case for providing district judges with the power to appoint special prosecutors to aid in various investigations.

Where there is a conflict of interest, where high officials of the government are under investigation, or where the opponents of these high officials in previous elections are under that investigation, then I think a special counsel to a grand jury would be very useful. This argument seems particularly persuasive since Congress appears to be in a mood to pass laws regulating elections, to pass laws which would greatly increase the chance of political trials taking place in the United States in the future.

In my opinion the special counsel ought not to have the power to prosecute. I think that decision should remain in the Department of Justice, that the indictment should be signed by the U.S. attorney and that, if the U.S. attorney declines to sign it, the judge could make the presentment public to the people. Again, the ultimate decision would be political, subject to political sanctions if the Justice Department decided not to go ahead and there was a strong case.

But there are also cases in our recent history in which district judges have tried to get local U.S. attorneys to prosecute civil rights demonstrators and in which the Justice Department was clearly right in declining to prosecute.

So I think there is a good argument for a reform here —although I feel the tremor of dissent to my right, at least on the issues of a special prosecutor.

MR. BICKEL: Well, to say that your suggestion is an overreaction to Watergate is to put it mildly, and to say that it's probably unconstitutional is just to add, I think, icing to the cake. I am opposed to the idea.

I don't know what our political scientist friends think about it. I'll just suggest to them, because this ought to hit a nerve, that at the very least this would establish— whether it's a permanent, independent special prosecutor or nearly 500 district judges all over the country with the power to appoint special prosecutors at will—would establish serious power, major power, in irresponsible hands, in hands that are accountable to no one.

And I should think if there's any single thing about the genius of our government and the fundamental meaning of separation of powers, really, it is that there is no such thing as power anywhere in government which is unaccountable to anybody, except for the adjudicative function of the judiciary. Otherwise, power is either legislative or executive, not because it's elegant to divide power that way, but because those are two categories of accountability, of power running from whoever exercises it, ultimately, to democratic responsibility.

MR. SCAMMON: Except in the case of the courts.

MR. BICKEL: Well, yes.

MR. SCAMMON: I would think, Alex, that one would have to recognize, particularly in the last decade of actions, that courts quite frequently are placed willy-nilly in the role of making law and yet, at the federal level at least, no one has seriously proposed that judges be elected for a limited term and then be subject to reelection.

MR. BICKEL: But the critique of judicial activism always is bottomed in the end, fundamentally, on this proposition. The trouble with judges making law, rather than deciding cases and making whatever law they make only interstitially for purposes of disposing of that case, is that it is irresponsible power.

MR. WILSON: Let me make the case more strongly. If you look at the behavior of many federal district court judges, you can only conclude that significant numbers of them have decided to appoint themselves school superintendent, zoning commissioner, health commissioner, consumer representative and ecological czar. Now the suggestion is that in addition they appoint themselves district attorney and chief of police. I think that the line should have been drawn back a ways. But this is probably as good a place as any to dig in our heels.

This does not mean, however, that I'm opposed to the idea of a special prosecutor. I think for all of the reasons that Ralph Winter indicated, there are circumstances in which we have to have a genuinely independent prosecutor. And though I have no particular proposal to make, I'd like to ask Ralph why he is suggesting that the prosecutor be selected by district judges instead of through some congressional procedure whereby Congress, with the consent of both houses—perhaps outside of the normal committee structure, because we do not want the committees to be not only investigative bodies but also prosecutive bodies—could under certain circumstances select special prosecutors. Or is that power already so well recognized that no special provision is necessary?

MR. WINTER: I think Congress can call for the appointment of a special prosecutor. It can pass legislation. But that is too unwieldy; it involves too much political controversy and the like surrounding the investigation.

I prefer a system in which district judges would have the power to appoint the special counsel. I would permit the Justice Department to appeal. The special counsel could run an investigation, and the political sanction would come into play when the presentment is made.

MR. BICKEL: Do you know what enormous power you would be lodging in them? It's the power of sitting there with a grand jury, which, of course, the prosecutor directs. The grand jury doesn't exist, really, aside from the prosecutor. The prosecutor has the power to subpoena anybody he likes, to investigate anything he wants, to harrass, to pull people in, and then to issue a presentment and accuse people in public without the possibility of their defending themselves.

It's just an enormous power. People have been hollering and crying about the abuses of grand juries for years now, about the great irresponsible power they hold, and this has occurred when the grand jury has been, after all, a tool of a district attorney or a U.S. attorney who is politically responsible to someone. Now, you would cut that loose and let any district judge anywhere in the country appoint himself a fellow to wield that power.

That seems to be an absolute enormity.

MR. WINTER: Well, if you think grand juries have too much power, then we ought to be talking about reforming grand juries. I'm talking about—

MR. BICKEL: You're talking about giving them more power.

MR. WINTER: No, I'm not. I'm talking about giving them a device to help them operate more effectively. In the other areas we have discussed, we have tried to find some kind of institutional arrangement that would impose a heavy political sanction upon those who engage in various abuses. That sanction is not very strong in the pre-investigation stage. In fact, I think the possibility of abuse is much greater in the pre-investigation stage than it is further on in the process.

You know, the whole way in which the Watergate situation broke does tend to indicate that it's very hard to carry on an effective investigation of high officials in the

61

government. It's hard for everybody in the Justice Department, it's hard for the prosecutors, it's hard for the witnesses, it's hard for everybody.

MR. WELLINGTON: Perhaps one of the lessons of Watergate, as it will turn out, is that the ad hoc appointment of a special prosecutor by the attorney general is a successful device for the extraordinary case.

Part of my difficulty with Ralph's proposal is that it works at cross purposes with what I think is an essential reform, namely, the real strengthening of the Justice Department. The attorney general and the appointed assistants must be men of very high professional quality. Moreover, career lawyers in the Justice Department must be men and women of quality and their jobs must be regarded as of high status in the legal profession. I think that we haven't done enough in this direction. Part of the fault lies with the law schools. Many law students believe that it would be a good idea to work in a U.S. attorney's office or in the Justice Department for a short period of time—good training before going into private practice. We ought to pay career attorneys better. We ought to increase their status.

I think that if we were to have regular special prosecutors, we would lower the status of the Justice Department lawyer. This would be demoralizing. Many good people who might otherwise find a career in the Justice Department would find working there unacceptable. They would be out of the big cases; the implication would be that they could not be trusted.

MR. BICKEL: You know, it can be done—just to interrupt for a minute. For some decades now, the office of the solicitor general has been a career office in which people of high status in the profession serve for years on end— ten, fifteen years. Why can't that be done in other parts of the Justice Department?

MR. WELLINGTON: Well, I think there are some cases where it has occurred. Certainly Mr. Peterson is an example.

MR. BICKEL: Yes.

MR. WELLINGTON: But it doesn't always happen, and it should be encouraged. Certainly the notion of removing the Justice Department from the executive branch and making it independent seems to me to be unquestionably wrong.

MR. WILSON: Ludicrous is the word you're searching for. [Laughter.]

MR. WINTER: I want to dissent from the proposition that it would lower the morale of professional lawyers in the Justice Department to have this kind of provision around. In my view they would like it and they would use it. I think it would free them from the very dangerous procedure we now have of their filing a piece of paper that's printed in the Code of Federal Regulations saying what a special prosecutor's jurisdiction is, so that the special prosecutor is constantly put at odds with the Justice Department over that jurisdiction and in a position where he has to fight it. I think such a proposal would be welcomed by a professionalized staff in the Justice Department and would not lower their morale.

This is not to say that I don't want a professionalized staff. One thing we've got to do is stop appointing campaign managers to the post of attorney general. We've just got to stop that. All administrations, whether Republican or Democratic, have been doing it. It's a terrible mistake; it's an invitation to trouble because it gives us attorney generals with too many partisan responsibilities.

MR. BICKEL: We used to make them postmaster general and you saw what happened. And now we make them a—

MR. WILSON: They couldn't deliver the mail and now we put them in the Justice Department. [Laughter.]

MR. BICKEL: I'd like to return to a point Harry touched on which I think deserves emphasis. What is it in the experience of Watergate, in the experience of corruption and scandals in the Truman administration, of some scandals in the Eisenhower administration, then back to Teapot Dome—what is it that persuades you that political pressures don't work perfectly well to solve the problem of the Justice Department's sort of prosecuting itself?

Under Harry Truman, there was an episode with a special prosecutor. He went out, but prosecutions went on very nicely. T. Lamar Caudle served his term in jail—et cetera, et cetera. In the case of Teapot Dome, a method for appointing a special prosecutor, two special prosecutors, subject to Senate confirmation was worked out and they prosecuted all you want. In the current instance, with all of the pressures of Watergate, that's the one difficulty that was met: the special prosecutor's office has worked.

MR. SCAMMON: Alex, aren't you really, though, raising the nice question—what those of you of the legal discipline are really afraid of, it seems to me, is that the special prosecutor will cease to become special and will become sort of normal. He will become, in the best sense of the word, a pursuer of people—ranging all over the horizon, doing anything he wants, ceasing to be special in the sense that he's named for a special purpose for a limited period and then gets out. And, like many other bureaucrats, he will stay on and on, ad infinitum, ad nauseum, until pretty soon the whole operation has become a vast legion of special prosecutors.

Is that a fair statement—maybe a little overblown—but is it fair?

MR. BICKEL: Yes. That's a perfectly fair point. It's more applicable to a permanent special prosecutor, and I think it's even worse than you say. If we had a permanent special prosecutor and he were there to deal with corruption and misdeeds, the first thing he'd be doing would be to institutionalize the cynicism which exists anyway—the notion that government is full of crooks. You'd be saying, "Yes, that's right. Government is full of crooks and we need somebody to ride shotgun on the flanks of any administration because all administrations are full of crooks."

Now, that is a terrible thing to do—to institutionalize peoples' cynicism.

And if it weren't a permanent special prosecutor but one of these roving types appointed by district judges all over the country, it would amount to the same thing. Every ambitious district judge, you know—it runs through the mind—Which week of the year would Gerhardt Gesell not appoint a special prosecutor? Which week of the year would Judge Harold Cox of Mississippi not have appointed a special prosecutor to investigate lying and misprision of felony and miscarriage of justice on the part of the Justice Department in civil rights cases or abuse of white peoples' civil rights by the FBI? Which week of the year would he not have had a special prosecutor?

MR. SCAMMON: It just seems to me an absolutely appalling—

MR. BICKEL:—proposal, which, however, we ought to consider seriously. [Laughter.]

MR. SCAMMON: But it also seems to me—again, if I may speak for you, what it seems to me you're saying is that the further the actions of government are removed from the electoral control of the people, the more likely they are to ride roughshod over the rights of the people. And at the federal level, the life term conferred upon the judge, with removal only under the most heinous of circumstances, does inevitably lead to a certain distance between him and the people.

Now, perhaps this is wise in the administration of justice. But I can see your point entirely—that to sort of equip each judge with an extra-duty mace, which seems to be how you regard the special prosecutor—would have consequences that Ralph wouldn't agree with, but—

MR. WINTER: Well, now wait a second—

MR. BICKEL: Suppose a special prosecutor had been appointed, as he undoubtedly would have been if this proposal had been on the books, during the McCarthy era when Joe McCarthy was saying: "The Truman administration is full of spies. The President isn't prosecuting his own people. Alger Hiss is Dean Acheson's friend, this is all one circle, and he's not cleaning it up. We need a special prosecutor to get in there." And so Otto Otepka or somebody gets appointed special prosecutor until he finishes the case. He'd still be there prosecuting Red spies today because, though the mood has changed, as has the politics of the country, he'd be independent of it and he'd be out there after the Reds. He'd be doing it today.

MR. WELLINGTON: Well, in defense of Ralph—

MR. WINTER: Gee, I wouldn't mind it if you guys would let me defend myself. But, go ahead, Harry. [Laughter.]

MR. WELLINGTON: Now, some of the exaggerated consequences of Ralph's proposal might be cured if one were to set about drafting a statute dealing with his proposal. I don't mean to suggest that on balance I think it's a good proposal, but I think it's something to be considered dispassionately.

We might just say a word about the Constitution.

MR. BICKEL: Yes, I was going to say, I don't want to bore you with legal technicalities, but there are serious constitutional problems.

MR. WELLINGTON: Right, and that might be a reason for rejecting Ralph's proposal. I believe what I take it you and Ralph and even political scientists probably believe, namely, that there is an obligation in Congress to consider constitutional questions. Surely where the wisdom of legislation is unclear, legislators should stay their hand—if they think their handiwork might raise a serious constitutional question.

MR. BICKEL: And a serious constitutional question, in a nutshell, is what is assumed away by Ralph, namely, whether prosecution is an executive or judicial function.

MR. WILSON: Who is this Ralph we keep talking about? [Laughter.] Is there such a person?

MR. BICKEL: A man named Winter. He's a sunshine soldier.

MR. WINTER: He's alive and well somewhere.

If I may, Alex, assume you away for a minute, I think there is abundant authority to appoint a special prosecutor. There is a provision in the Constitution saying that Congress may empower the courts to appoint various federal officers—

MR. BICKEL: For example, secretary of state.

MR. WINTER: As you know, I say in the pamphlet that they can't do that. But they can appoint officers connected with the judicial function. This is connected with the judicial function.

MR. BICKEL: That's the question. That's the issue.

MR. WINTER: A special prosecutor has only investigative power; he does not have the power to prosecute.

MR. BICKEL: The investigative power is not a judicial power.

MR. WINTER: Nor do I see, Alex, why this particular power cannot be surrounded by safeguards like a requirement to find a probable cause or other things like that. You know, I—

MR. BICKEL: Shifting around.

MR. WINTER: —think it's ridiculous to say that there would be 500 special prosecutors, that every district judge would have his own special prosecutor—

MR. BICKEL: No, there would be more than 500, because the number of district judges is rising. There would be many more.

But you see how you beg the question. Sure, if this is a judicial investigation—

MR. WINTER: I wish I had a chance to beg the question. [Laughter.]

MR. BICKEL: You wrote the book. [Laughter.]

If it were true that investigation and prosecution were judicial functions, then I would agree the Constitution does say Congress may empower the courts to make such appointments. But I read that power as limited to judicial or near-judicial functions, although two cases have mistakenly gone farther, and that would be fine.

But the gut issue is whether prosecution and investigation are judicial functions. You argue beautifully, in arguing against an independent Department of Justice, that investigation and prosecution are executive functions. I think that's true and I think that's constitutionally true and I think, therefore, there would be the most serious constitutional problem—

MR. WINTER: Where do the Securities and Exchange Commission and the National Labor Relations Board get their powers to investigate? They're independent; they're not controlled by the executive branch. Your argument is against all of the administrative agencies—wipe them out. Not that that's such a bad argument.

MR. BICKEL: Well, that's the scenic route of last night.

The place of the administrative agency in the constitutional scheme, while somewhat dubious to begin with, is not what you would propose for these special prosecutors. These would be fellows appointed by the President and confirmed by the Senate. They would exercise quasi-judicial functions in one part of them, which makes them judges. You can appoint judges and call them SEC commissioners or you can appoint judges and call them judges.

MR. WINTER: The SEC has a lot to do about prosecuting people.

MR. BICKEL: They would exercise, on the other hand, some noncriminal prosecutorial functions. That function is separated from the quasi-judicial function in some administrative agencies, and strong arguments have been made that it ought to be separated in all of them, that it's a mistake to weld them.

And they would also exercise what are viewed as legislative functions—filling in details by delegation from Congress of legislation and administering the legislation.

Now, people had a lot of trouble with that when it was first set up 100 years ago, and one might want to rethink that. It's too late to rethink it, but it's certainly no argument, no handle for you, to leap from the SEC to the different and aggravated constitutional monstrosity of prosecutors appointed by Judges Harold Cox and Gerhardt Gesell.

MR. WINTER: It seems to me that the SEC's having the power, as you describe it, to act as judge, to act as prosecutor, to act as legislator—that that is a far greater offense against your view of the Constitution than the kind of very limited proposal I made.

The special counsel I'm talking about wouldn't even have the power to prosecute. And, as you well know, Alex, and have not revealed to the audience—thereby violating the Security and Exchange Act of 1935—the states have a long, historical background of special prosecutors.

MR. BICKEL: Well, states do all kinds of things; they mix all kinds of powers. I don't think the law of Connecticut binds the U.S. Constitution.

But at the very least, there's a serious constitutional problem. It ought to give Congress pause and at least lead it to consider the equally serious policy and prudential questions that have been raised by everybody else against your isolated position.

MR. WINTER: That merely shows who is the true reformer on the Yale Law School faculty. [Laughter.]

MR. WILSON: If I have time, Mr. Chairman, could I emphasize one aspect of our consideration of the Justice

Department that I think many people have misunderstood. In thinking about the Justice Department, we often see areas of success where, in fact, there are weaknesses or failures and areas of failure where, in fact, there are strengths. I think it's much easier for the layman to draw erroneous conclusions about Watergate with respect to the Justice Department than with respect to other areas, because it's a complex organization and has, to be charitable, rather obscure functions in the layman's mind.

For example, many people think that the system of United States attorneys is a good idea because one of them obtained an indictment of Mr. Mitchell, Mr. Stans and Mr. Vesco. I happen to think that that's not a revelation of the strength of the system, but an accidental feature of a system that is on the whole rather bad. We do not have, as Mr. Wellington said, a serious professional development of trained lawyers in capacities as U.S. attorneys and assistant U.S. attorneys. What we have is a group of men who work for United States senators. They don't work for the President, and they don't work for the attorney general.

Others may conclude that the Justice Department mismanages the Antitrust Division because they think of antitrust prosecution as a perpetual motion machine, as something you can wind up and put on a track and it goes around automatically. Actually, the most important economic and political judgments have to be made about what kind of case you want to prosecute. It seems to me that the intervention of the President and the attorney general in the ITT case is entirely correct in a legal sense. That is to say, they have every right to raise serious political and economic questions, especially economic questions, as to whether breaking up ITT makes any sense or not. Whether they do it out of proper or improper motives is the important question.

But, from much of the popular discussion, one gets the impression that what we need is an automatic Justice Department, a little Lionel train that goes around on a track and that prosecutes every conspiracy to restrain trade and every organized crime racketeer and that arrests every heroin dealer. That is not at all the way the system can work or should work. This as much as anything leads me to believe that not only is the notion of an independent Justice Department wrong, but so is the notion that the Justice Department as now organized and managed is one of the strengths of the system.

MR. BICKEL: Well, I think Harry was saying that we need to raise its professional standards. The thing that has been wrong with elevating political managers to attorney general is that, with the sole exception of Robert Kennedy, they haven't brought in good people. That kind of attorney general has tended, with exceptions, to bring in at the sub-cabinet level politicians and not professionals—certainly not people with standing in the profession. That's bad.

But that is not to say that the Justice Department ought to be outside of political control. Of course, it has to be politically controlled. In fact, that's one of the difficulties with Ralph's proposal, because even the kind of case that he would give to a special prosecutor raises issues of the same sort, political issues. The Agnew case is an example.

MR. WILSON: Nothing I can do short of streaking will get attention away from—[Laughter.] I will draw the line.

MR. BICKEL: Well, the Agnew case would be a typical special prosecutor case, wouldn't it?

MR. WILSON: Yes.

MR. BICKEL: And in that case a political judgment had to be made. I think a correct one was made in the end—namely, to take a plea bargain from him, to allow him to resign. That is a decision that oughtn't to be made by anybody who has no connection to political responsibility, who is not answerable to somebody who is in turn answerable to the people. It would be just inconceivable.

I think it's certainly true that if you let things go as they are, you are expecting, in situations of this sort, that the administration will prosecute itself.

As the President demonstrated when he fired Cox and as he would demonstrate if he fired Jaworski (if he were to take *that* political risk), there's no way to run the executive department outside his control. But for God's sake, I think it's been demonstrated where the countervailing power is and how effective it can be. Namely, it's in Congress. In other words, the President does enough of that and he runs the risk of impeachment. Harry Truman fired Newbold Morris, but he didn't go so far as to try to quash the prosecution of those who had done wrong. If he had, he would have been impeached or he would have at least had a Senate select committee on his back. That's where the countervailing power is, and that's the genius of our system.

I'd like to end with these stirring remarks, but first I ought to give Ralph one more rebuttal.

MR. WINTER: That's all right.

MR. BICKEL: Well, then, I think we've covered this relatively uncontroversial subject with a satisfying consensus among the members of the panel—[Laughter]—and we therefore approach the last part of our program in a proper spirit. Having achieved unity on this subject, perhaps we can go on to even greater unity on the next.

OUR LAST TOPIC TONIGHT concerns problems that are of immediate current interest and are on everybody's mind. They are these: What is an impeachable offense, and do we need a comprehensive, theoretical definition of it?

What is the reach of the impeachment power of the House of Representatives as far as obtaining evidence is concerned?

How does that impeachment power exert itself, perhaps by subpoena, against a claim of executive privilege?

Does it override it? Are there any limits to the House investigative power in an impeachment process, and who decides this issue? The House for itself? Do the courts have any role? Is it an impeachable offense in itself to withhold information that the House demands in an impeachment process?

What about the House making public in the course of impeachment proceedings evidence that might, or is claimed to, prejudice defendants in a criminal trial? Again, may a court control that—that is, may it in some fashion try to prevent the House from engaging in proceedings that are thought to prejudice the rights of defendants?

This is the bag of problems that is now confronting the House of Representatives, the White House and, in some measure, the courts.

Since Ralph Winter's report has a discussion of executive privilege, let's start out with him on this issue as well.

MR. WINTER: I think the impeachment question does call upon us to make a distinction between what is an impeachable offense justifying removal after trial in the Senate and what is an impeachable offense justifying judicial enforcement of a subpoena issue by the House in the course of undertaking its responsibility to investigate with a view to impeachment. I would hate to see the courts get involved in the first question. I would hate to see them being called upon to define what kinds of acts justify the Congress in impeaching and removing the President and then, I suppose, in reviewing the evidence.

I also think that there really are no standards for impeachment. We are in the midst of a debate as to whether the standard is an abuse of power, a gross abuse of power, or only indictable offenses.

It seems to me that in terms of raw power, the Congress has the power to impeach and to remove for more or less whatever cause it wants to. It shouldn't do that. It should impeach only for gross abuses, in my view. It also seems to me that you can't limit it to indictable offenses. If we elect a President who one day wakes up and says—"Gosh, I've got a nice place in the islands; I'll see you guys around"—and just walks out, I think our Constitution provides a means of handling that situation.

The more difficult problem comes, I think, when the House votes and seeks to enforce subpoenas in a court—more difficult because courts are bound by a standard of legal relevancy. I myself think that most congressional demands for information from the President are not enforceable. They are not, as lawyers would say, justiciable. In other words, a court should not recognize the claim of executive privilege so much as it should decline to adjudicate the issue.

The reason for this is that congressional demands for information, congressional subpoenas, are based quite as much on political considerations as they are on a need for the data for the purposes of considering legislation. Similarly, the President's refusal to grant the information is a mix of political considerations and of a desire to maintain the privacy of presidential discussions. I don't know how a court can weigh these political considerations.· I think political considerations ought to be determined by politics. Congress ought to mobilize public opinion; the President ought to mobilize public opinion; and wherever the political sanctions fall, that's how it turns out. If the public really wants the President to produce all the information the executive branch has to offer, it can elect a President who will do that.

I distinguish this from a grand jury subpoena. Where the grand jury subpoena is concerned, a judge can make a decision as to relevancy to a particular crime, as to the need for the information, the availability of alternative sources, and a lot of other things that he can't make where congressional subpoenas are concerned. I find myself far more favorable to the enforcement of grand jury subpoenas where there are proper safeguards—sworn testimony that specified evidence contains relevant information, and the like.

Impeachment, it seems to me, falls between these. In thinking about it—and I'd like to hear what my colleagues think about this—I come down as follows: When the claimed impeachable offense is of a noncriminal nature, subpoenas are nonjusticiable. Where the subpoena charges an offense that is an indictable offense, a court might well say this is like a grand jury subpoena. In the latter case, impeachment of a President is a substitute for indictment of a President, and I think the need for enforcement is much greater there. But, again, it has to be specific evidence, sworn testimony that the evidence contains matters relevant to the offense. It ought not to be some kind of general claim of power to the indexes of all presidential papers and all presidential assistants' papers and the right to go through those files without restriction. That, it seems to me, is impermissible.

If we had a rule like that, we would set ourselves up— if I may borrow a tactic of my colleagues, in discovering that my proposal for a special counsel would lead to over 500 special counsels—for repeated impeachment inquiries, so-called impeachment inquiries, with a subpoena demanding access to files. I think we might seriously and permanently damage the presidency if we don't restrict in some way, ·if we don't build safeguards around congressional subpoenas, even where there are impeachment proceedings under way.

MR. BICKEL: Though obviously wounded by the reception to his last set of proposals, Ralph has rescued his good common sense and returned to his paths. [Laughter.]

I generally agree. I would not draw the line at offenses that are criminal, indictable offenses.

I certainly agree. It seems to me the text of the Constitution is plain on it—that there can't be judicial review of the impeachment process, that there can't be an appeal from the impeachment judgment in the Senate to the Supreme Court, in effect, for the Court to pass on the validity of the impeachment. I think the Constitution just says to the contrary.

On the other hand, that doesn't mean, as Ralph says, that when it comes to a subpoena the judges are equally excluded. It doesn't mean that, for one thing, because the alternative to involving the judicial process in some measure is to force Congress to drop the atom bomb, is to force

75

Congress to say that any denial, any refusal to accede to a request for information, is in itself an impeachable offense. That seems to me a resolution of the problem that is of a magnitude and of a violence, if you will, which is undesirable. So, I think, although the inclination seems to be to the contrary in the House now, that the House ought to go to a judge with its subpoenas.

Now, what is the judge to do? Sure, the case is easy if the information is relevant to an indictable offense. If it is not, it seems to me the judge cannot avoid asking himself the question, "Is the information relevant to what would properly be an impeachable offense?" You see, while as a matter of raw power the House can impeach for anything, the fact is that it shouldn't and that there ought to be limits on the impeachment power, very serious limits, because otherwise ours will become a parliamentary system of government.

A judge ought to ask that question. I think if it is plain in his mind that the information is not relevant to an impeachable offense, for example, if the House now asks for information on the President's practice of impounding funds—a dubious constitutional practice perhaps, but surely not an impeachable offense—in such an event, I think a judge ought to say, "I will not enforce that subpoena."

If it is a marginal matter, then perhaps the judge ought to give the House the benefit of the doubt and enforce it, even though the offense charged is not an indictable offense. For example, suppose the President has been found to have pursued the practice of assigning FBI agents to shadow every congressman and every senator and of not necessarily tapping their telephones, but exercising enormous amounts of surveillance over their activities. This is not a criminal offense, but I think it is certainly an abuse of power that ought to be an impeachable offense. It seems to me that a judge ought to issue a subpoena for information relevant to that kind of a charge, as much as for information relevant to a charge of obstruction of justice, or what have you.

So, I would place the judge in an arbitrating position, in order to make it less likely that Congress will enforce its subpoenas by impeachment itself, and in order to have at this preliminary stage some control over the impulse to use the impeachment power in unbridled fashion—which is an impulse, if we allow it to proceed to its satisfaction, that would destroy the separation of powers and make the President simply a creature of Congress.

MR. WELLINGTON: I would like to disagree in part, if I may. Certainly I don't want to disagree with the proposition that the House should be very careful and circumspect in deciding what constitutes an impeachable offense. But I am concerned about the House going to a court and asking it to enforce a subpoena. I am concerned quite simply because of separation of powers.

I can see the merit of the contrary position. It sounds like a nice accommodation. The trouble is, however, that it erodes the political question doctrine.

First, imagine, if you will, an order by a district court judge enforcing a subpoena, and imagine the order being appealed. Perhaps it will finally reach the Supreme Court. Remember that if we do have an impeachment trial, the chief justice of the Supreme Court sits over the Senate. This troubles me.

Second, I don't know how a court writes an opinion. What does it say about why it is or is not enforcing a subpoena that doesn't very seriously intrude on what I would take the Constitution to impower the House to decide, namely, what is an impeachable offense?

I think it is a very hard problem. I don't like saying that the court shouldn't be involved in it—it's such a nice-seeming accommodation—but it seems to me that judicial enforcement of a House subpoena in an impeachment proceeding is the paradigmatic example of the political question.

MR. BICKEL: Well, it's political enough. The Constitution says the House has the sole power to vote a bill of impeachment.

MR. WELLINGTON: That's right.

MR. BICKEL: And it says the Senate tries. It doesn't say anything about how you get information.

MR. WELLINGTON: I understand.

MR. BICKEL: The real problem is that these two things overlap, and that you can't decide the information question without—

MR. WELLINGTON: Right.

MR. BICKEL: —having something to say about the nature of the impeachment power. You only say that in connection with your subpoena. Whatever you say makes no inroads at all upon the House's ultimate power to impeach and the Senate's ultimate power to try, which stand as nonjusticiable.

MR. WELLINGTON: But doesn't it substantially influence what the House then will do—

MR. BICKEL: It may.

MR. WELLINGTON: —and doesn't the court then play a very important role in deciding what constitutes an impeachable offense? If so, it is contrary to the spirit of the Constitution.

MR. BICKEL: It may, but it is an accommodation, I think, to which one is led by an absolute horror of the opposite result. Because the opposite result would be that you could probably turn almost anything into an impeachable offense by asking for information, issuing your subpoena and, when the President denied it, you'd have an impeachable offense.

MR. WELLINGTON: But we haven't had much of a history of—

MR. WILSON: None at all.

MR. BICKEL: Well, no we haven't, but we are starting into—

MR. WELLINGTON: Why should we assume that that's going to be the future?

MR. WINTER: Isn't that kind of history more likely once you open up the judicial remedy? Once you open up the judicial remedy, you are issuing an invitation to Congress to go after information it couldn't otherwise get.

For example, in the Kennedy administration during the missile crisis, there were allegations—if I'm recalling it incorrectly, take it as a hypothetical case—there were allegations that well before President Kennedy went on television the evidence was quite strong that missiles had been introduced into Cuba. I think the evidence was based not only on espionage within Cuba but upon indications that the freighters observed going to Cuba were of a kind that probably could carry only missiles. It may well be an impeachable offense for the President of the United States to delay and then take the kind of action Kennedy took on the eve of an election. I think somebody might well consider that a gross abuse of power, according to the House staff report that—

MR. BICKEL: You mean he exercises power as commander-in-chief, and is—

MR. WINTER: Just suppose that—

MR. BICKEL: It's like submitting as an impeachable offense the fact that the Battle of the Bulge took place.

MR. WINTER: No, no. Suppose there is an allegation that the timing and the content of an action that a President takes—I'm not saying that it happened—the timing and the content is governed entirely by partisan political considerations. That seems to me to fall within the definition of impeachment that the House staff report talks about.

MR. BICKEL: It is much too broad.

MR. WINTER: Well, I'm not so sure that's true.

MR. BICKEL: I would say that a subpoena directed at impoundment or, to give you another example, a subpoena directed at the bombing in Cambodia—I would assume that a court would simply not have anything to do with those subpoenas—

MR. WINTER: Why?

MR. BICKEL: —because it would say those are outer reaches of the impeachment power which are, at the very least, so dubious that it will not lend its authority.

MR. WINTER: How do we know that they are dubious?

MR. BICKEL: Well, we decide they are dubious.

MR. WINTER: On what ground? Take Harry's question. What opinion does the court write? What does the court say? What standards does it apply in determining this?

MR. BICKEL: What you are saying is that we have no standards for defining the impeachment power. I think that is quite wrong. I think the beginning of a definition of what is the proper reach of the impeachment power is the nature of this government, separation of powers and the independence of the President. Lots of history bears on this. We posit the impossibility of maintaining that separation and that independence if political errors, if all kinds of misdeeds and dubious interpretations of the Constitution, are impeachable offenses. Then the President becomes responsible to Congress after the fashion of a prime minister.

MR. WINTER: I agree.

MR. BICKEL: Now, that is a theory that is just as good— in fact, it is a lot better and can lead to a lot closer reasoning than many a theory on which courts decide cases. I think it is nonjusticiable for courts to apply this theory once Congress has run amuck and gone wrong, impeached the President, and even convicted him. There is no review.

But, on the issue of a subpoena, I don't see why a court can't figure out what an impeachable offense is on the basis of this kind of reasoning and say, "This subpoena will issue. The other one won't. If you want to go and run it politically, we can't stop you, but you can't have the aid of the judicial power in enforcing that kind of a subpoena."

MR. WILSON: Why do we assume that the courts, whom we've previously described as 500 district court judges running around changing the zoning laws and appointing prosecutors to investigate the NAACP, are or should be a reasonable check on the impeachment process?

We've only had one impeachment, and that did not lead to a conviction. We have had no other serious efforts to impeach the President.

It seems to me that the principal check on the impeachment process is the political position of Congress vis-à-vis the public and the presidency. Congress, far from having rushed headlong into premature impeachment, has moved—to put it mildly—with majestic stateliness, accompanied by a good deal of frivolous bickering on the side.

What we really object to are some of the more dubious, but altogether to be expected, staff reports, public speeches, and gallery-pleasing declamations of those of who would like to get Richard Nixon for everything from Tricia's wedding to the Cambodian incursion, from ITT to Watergate. But, I see no support for those sentiments in the Congress as a whole. And I think that Congress, which is composed of practical men and women with substantial political experience, is aware of the enormous respect the American people have for the office of the presidency, the enormous respect they have for established procedures.

It has taken severe jolts to get public opinion to even consider that we may be in a desperate position, and there is still no general public support for the notion of impeachment. There is a support, perhaps, for a change of some sort if it could be arrived at by a process to which the word impeachment did not apply. I think that that is going to be a continuing feature of the American political system, because these attitudes to which Congress is responding—not in a nakedly self-serving way, because I think Congress shares these attitudes—are not attitudes of the moment.

I think Dick Scammon would say that opinion polls and surveys, going back as far as we have them, indicate this enormous reservoir of deference, almost amounting—if I may shift the metaphor—to an inertial force that supports the institutions of government. It is best illustrated in the field of foreign policy. The American public never wants to go to war. All opinion polls show we should stay out of Vietnam, stay out of Israel, stay out of Europe, stay out of the Far East. The same polls always show that the public will support the President in whatever he does, including taking us to war in any of those places. And the support will last for a long period of time—not indefinitely, but for a long period of time.

That, it seems to me, is the crucial political reality around which these constitutional issues are revolving.

MR. SCAMMON: Alex, if I may add my voice to that of my fellow political scientist, in opposition to the battery of legal talent—

MR. WELLINGTON: No, I was on your side.

MR. SCAMMON: I know you were. [Laughter.]

MR. WILSON: We're going to make you an honorary member. [Laughter.]

MR. SCAMMON: I think it is basically correct that when you talk about impeachment what you are talking about is a political action with respect to the presidency that many people view with revulsion. It is not easy to bring off. It has been tried, and the public hasn't given the idea very high marks. It really is the reverential awe in which people hold the presidency as a general institution that is the best check of all.

I do think also, Alex, that your point in response to Mr. Wellington is a sound one. If you do carry through a successful impeachment, you're never going to be a virgin again. In other words, the third attempt would be a lot easier, and maybe then we would be approaching something of a parliamentary government. But one must also remember that in a parliamentary government the head of state also has the right to dissolve the legislature.

MR. BICKEL: So it would be a flaw in parliamentary government.

MR. SCAMMON: So how many congressmen would really want to move into a situation in which their heads would go on the block en masse whenever the President decided it would be a good thing to dissolve Congress and have new elections.

MR. BICKEL: But they wouldn't.

MR. SCAMMON: That's right.

MR. BICKEL: But none—

MR. SCAMMON: But I think it is a long jump from one successful impeachment, if it were successful, to playing footsie with parliamentary systems of the government.

MR. BICKEL: Well, it does say that it is important to worry about what grounds this impeachment is placed on.

And as to the point that the ultimate recourse is to public opinion, and what have you, that is undoubtedly true as to the whole—

MR. SCAMMON: Alex, if I may interrupt, it is far more true with the Senate than with the House. Members of the House do have the get-away plank. They can all say, "Well, I want to have all the evidence brought out. So, in all conscience, I join with my colleagues in voting for an indictment. But my vote doesn't mean I say he is guilty."

MR. BICKEL: That's right.

MR. SCAMMON: But senators have to vote up or down on the guilt question.

MR. WILSON: By a two-thirds vote.

MR. SCAMMON: Yes—which is not easy.

The managers on the House side also want to present as solid a case as possible. They don't want to be accused of all sorts of high-handed practice and all sorts of hanky-panky in making their case. They want to make as good and as persuasive a case as they can, because it won't take more than a third of the Senate to keep that case from being a successful one, just as a third of the Senate kept the House from making a successful case 100 years ago against President Johnson.

MR. BICKEL: Well, I was going to say that I agree that the play of public opinion, that what the people are ready for, is decisive. It is decisive, I think, for the whole operation.

I don't think public opinion has the same weight on a specific request for information and the procedures by which the process goes forward or doesn't go forward. I don't think that public opinion—one way or the other, if ready for impeachment, or not ready for impeachment—is going to help you with that.

So, when it comes to a request of information in a subpoena, you've got a deadlock in the government, a deadlock which can be broken only by what I consider a rash and overreactive kind of thing. And the Congress might feel that it wants to break the deadlock that way because it's become a matter of institutional pride—you know, institutional machismo. One can see the beginning of that in the House today.

MR. SCAMMON: But Alex, you don't mean that—

MR. BICKEL: Maybe impeachment for not giving information. It is for that reason that I think one wants judges in there, inserted not to make policy and run school boards, but to perform what is quite properly a judicial function.

MR. SCAMMON: Alex, you are not really saying that there is an impasse. There is a way to break the impasse, namely, the Congress can vote the impeachment.

MR. BICKEL: Well, that's what I said.

MR. SCAMMON: What you are saying is for nondesirable—

MR. BICKEL: That's right.

MR. SCAMMON: But I think the basis for impeachment would have to be in the minds of the majority of the members in the Congress, the men who are going to manage the trial of the President before the Senate, and those who seek his conviction and removal from office. I don't think there is a member who is going to vote frivolously on this question.

MR. BICKEL: No, but they are put up to this choice: Either they may vote an impeachment, simply because of a denial of a request for information, and they may feel hot enough about that and be supported by the country in a general way, but perhaps not on the issue itself—which would be bad. Or they may withdraw and desist—which also would be bad. It is an impasse which I think is insoluble.

MR. WINTER: Alex, it is totally inconsistent with the position you were taking, I think, on special counsel to grand juries—[Laughter.]

MR. BICKEL: It really hurts, doesn't it?

MR. WINTER: In the case of special counsel, we have to fear the intervention of the 500 district judges, and political pressure would be enough. Here, you know, we are talking about impasse, and it can't be done, and atom bombs—

MR. BICKEL: Shall I explain it to you?

MR. WINTER: Well, I think you have already explained it—at great length as a matter of fact. [Laughter.]

MR. BICKEL: I know it still hurts. The wound is open. [Laughter.]

There you were talking about empowering a district judge, not responsible to anybody, on his own, to grab himself a prosecutor and a grand jury, and start roaming over the countryside with full investigative powers, and then issue a presentment, what have you, and bring power to bear on people, on individuals. Here we're talking about a judge sitting in the performance of a judicial function as a neutral agent, not self-starting, not investigating, not appointing anybody, but rather deciding what is a proper and customary judicial question: whether a subpoena is based on a sufficient claim of authority. Judges, of course, decide this question in every contempt-of-Congress case.

MR. WELLINGTON: Excuse me, but isn't there a difference in that the judge is not just deciding whether the subpoena is appropriate. He is also deciding what an impeachable offense is. He cannot decide whether it is appropriate to enforce a subpoena until he answers the second question of what is a constitutional ground for impeachment. I would maintain that that second question is none of his business.

MR. BICKEL: But, Harry, he doesn't conclude the second question. When he decides what is an impeachable offense, or that something is not an impeachable offense, that is not a decision that binds Congress so that Congress may not impeach for that offense.

MR. WELLINGTON: I understand that.

MR. BICKEL: He may influence them. But he doesn't decide that.

MR. WELLINGTON: I understand that.

MR. BICKEL: He is being asked to arbitrate and to help Congress in an exercise of power, where otherwise there is an impasse, soluble only in undesirable ways.

MR. WELLINGTON: But I would prefer—

MR. BICKEL: He can say, "I agree with Congress. This is an impeachable offense. I will help." If he says, "I disagree and I will not help," it is back to politics.

MR. WELLINGTON: No, he would say, "I don't agree with the committee that asks for this information."

MR. BICKEL: Right.

MR. WELLINGTON: Not with Congress.

MR. BICKEL: All right.

MR. WELLINGTON: I would prefer to leave the question to Congress, and I would prefer to allow the President's attorney to respond to that committee and explain why the White House would not produce the information. Let the committee then reach its conclusion about it, and put it to the House.

MR. BICKEL: Which does what?

MR. WELLINGTON: Does exactly what I would suppose a judge would do, but the House is empowered to do what a judge is not empowered to do.

MR. BICKEL: You've taken the House from a consideration of an impeachable offense which is obstruction of justice, and you've shifted the issue to an impeachable offense which is a failure to respond to a subpoena. And that becomes the impeachable offense, and that's what the House impeaches on. I think that is a very undesirable result.

MR. WILSON: But that isn't what happens. We are speaking as if we are confronting the first case in history in which a President of the United States may refuse information to a committee of Congress. Presidents of the United States refuse information to committees of Congress every year. That's what executive privilege is. That's what the refusal to allow presidential appointees under certain circumstances to testify amounts to.

And in all of these cases, Congress gets very mad. Its machismo is offended—or whatever the female equivalent of machismo is for Mrs. Abzug. [Laughter.] The members get indignant. They denounce, and they study the records of the Federal Convention. But they don't impeach. Why don't they impeach? Because they say, "Well, look, he has turned us down. He is a rascal. But it is not an impeachable matter."

Now we're assuming that in this case, because they are asking for information in connection with a potential impeachment inquiry—we're assuming that in this case, and this case only, they will get their dander up so that, without adequate grounds and in a frivolous way, they make an impeachment turn on the obstruction of justice. I'm not yet persuaded they will flip from their normal posture of frenzied impotence—and much of their frenzy is calculated because they know they are impotent—to one in which they will become malicious, that is, to try to impeach a President on weak grounds (which I believe would be a disaster) rather than on sound grounds.

If the President is going to be impeached and convicted, let us not repeat the history of the Warren Commission in which forever after we argue about whether it was the right thing to do or not. If we're going to do it, by God, let us do it, and on the most solid ground possible.

MR. BICKEL: Well, they may not turn that way. They may turn the other way and desist, which with their tendency to frenzied impotence is more likely. But that is bad, too.

What I am saying is that this issue, if allowed to be resolved by Congress, cannot be resolved well. It will be resolved in undesirable ways.

MR. WILSON: That's the nature of the system.

MR. BICKEL: And that's why—but the system also includes judges, whom we include when it comes to a grand jury subpoena.

MR. WILSON: I don't like judges.

MR. BICKEL: At all? [Laughter.]

MR. WELLINGTON: I like judges, and I want to save them.

MR. BICKEL: My understanding is that you are not a lawyer. [Laughter.]
Well, I take it we won't reach our last question, one which is currently facing Judge Sirica, namely, whether there is any possibility of a judge calling a halt, in effect, to any part of the impeachment proceeding because it prejudices criminal trials. I hope I stated the question so as to indicate the improbability of a judge acting that way. [Laughter.] And I freely predict that that is the conclusion that we would probably reach if we discussed this issue. However, we are—

MR. WELLINGTON: We could vote on it. [Laughter.]

MR. BICKEL: —out of time. So, I will close the proceedings now, thanking the panelists and the audience.